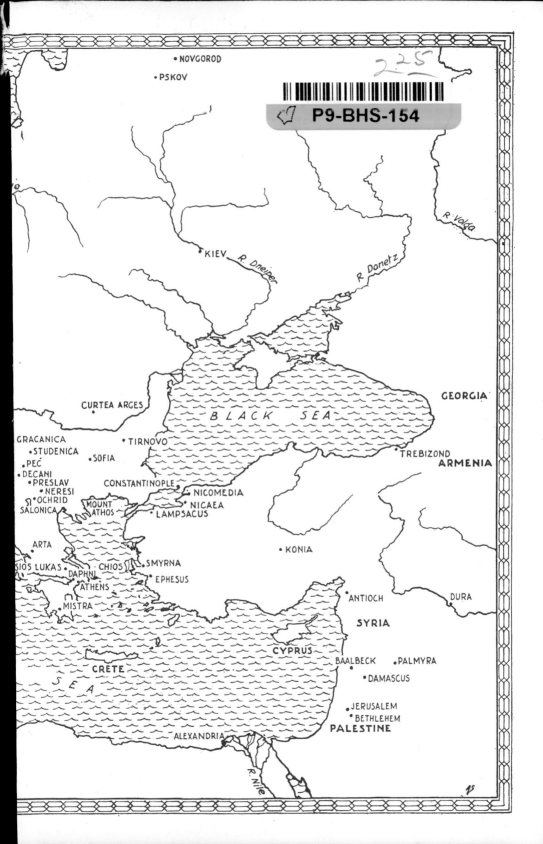

THE BEGINNINGS OF CHRISTIAN ART

Constantinople. Sancta Sophia. Christ from Deesis panel. Late twelfth century.
(*The Byzantine Institute.*)

THE BEGINNINGS
OF CHRISTIAN ART

By

D. TALBOT RICE

Watson-Gordon Professor of Fine Art
Edinburgh University

LONDON
HODDER & STOUGHTON

Made and Printed in Great Britain for
HODDER AND STOUGHTON LTD., by
T. AND A. CONSTABLE LTD., Printers,
Edinburgh

PREFACE

A SHORT time ago a very stimulating collection of essays was published under the title *History in a Changing World,* and in the first of them the author, Geoffrey Barraclough, laid stress on the necessity of reviewing our historical focus in order to cope with the new and wider horizon which world affairs have come to embrace. The old view, which was confined almost entirely to western Europe, provides, he suggests, a quite inadequate background, for to-day Russia, the Near East, the Islamic world and the Far East are just as much a part of the world in which we live as, say, Italy or Germany.

In the sphere of art, research in recent years has similarly enlarged our horizon, for it has disclosed on the one hand the immensity of the debt that the art of the Renaissance and of later times in the West owes to what went before, and on the other the importance, from a general point of view, of what was happening elsewhere, in regions which were in the past not taken into very much account.

This book has been written with that situation in mind. It deals with periods and subjects which are not generally familiar, and it aims at providing a background against which subsequent developments of Christian art can be properly studied. For that same reason particular attention is paid to the Byzantine world and to the role of Constantinople, for developments there were not only of the first importance but also continued without interruption from the early fourth to the fifteenth century, whereas elsewhere there was no such continuous achievement.

Another point is that of approach. The book is mainly about painting and mosaics, but the habit of treating the history of art as primarily the history of painting is not really a very commendable one. To be complete, the story of the art of any particular cultural phase should be concerned with every aspect, with sculpture as well as with painting, with the small things as well as with the large, and, not least, with architecture, which is just as much an expression of aesthetic thought and feeling as are the works that have apparently a far less functional purpose. This is particularly the case in the early mediaeval world, where buildings and their decoration constituted a very definite unity, and where the minor arts, ivory carvings, metal-work, textiles, enamels and pottery, had a significance that has now been forgotten in the West. But for the sake of convenience, and to keep books within bounds, architecture usually tends to be treated apart, and that practice has been followed here. Indeed, a very admirable general survey of that art already exists in Lethaby's *Mediaeval Art*. In addition, the reader is also referred for the early period to J. G. Davies, *The Origin and Development of Early Christian Church Architecture*, for the Byzantine world to J. A. Hamilton, *Byzantine Architecture and Decoration*, and for the West to A. W. Clapham's *Romanesque Architecture*.

The period covered in this book is that from the very begin-nings of Christianity till the time when a new outlook began to replace the early mediaeval one. In the West, north of the Alps, the change to this new way of thought began about the year 1100 and was completed by the change from the Romanesque to the Gothic style. In Italy the Romanesque style was never as important or as distinctive as it was in France, and it was separated by a much less definite barrier from what went before. The new age there thus hardly dawned as an independent one till towards the end of the thirteenth century, when Giotto began to develop what was eventually to become a new phase in the story of art. In the Byzantine world changes were, on the other hand, rather more rapid in early times, but later the pace was slower, and the old ideas continued to hold sway very much longer than in the West. In Greece and the Balkans, indeed, the old style survived almost intact even after the Turkish conquests of the fifteenth century, and good, though perhaps not great, works were still done in the old manner as late as the seven-teenth century. In Russia, too, the old style reigned until it was displaced by the westernising reforms of Peter the Great in the early eighteenth century. But the story of Russian art is an independent one, and it has been dealt with here briefly and with regard only to the earliest phases.

Most of the problems considered in this book have been

discussed in numerous specialised works, but these are more often than not in languages other than English, they are not always easily accessible, and are concerned with sections of the story only. But there have been a great many new discoveries over the last thirty years; numerous new ideas have been promulgated, and many new theories disseminated. The author has aimed at saying something about nearly all the more important of these discoveries and theories, and he hopes that his summary and comments may be of some use even to specialists. But the book, in dealing with early Christian and early mediaeval art as a whole, is intended primarily for the more general reader, and short bibliographies of essential or more easily accessible books where good illustrations or fuller surveys are to be found are included at the end of each chapter.

To these works may be added the names of a few more general ones which deal with the whole field and where there are full bibliographies. A. Grabar's *Byzantine Painting*, in the Skira series, is the most up-to-date work on painting and mosaic in the Byzantine world; E. W. Anthony's *Romanesque Frescoes* (Princeton, 1951) gives the full story of early painting in Italy and the West. Dalton's *East Christian Art* (Oxford, 1925) is the fullest and most authoritative manual; C. R. Morey's *Mediaeval Art* (New York, 1942) covers the entire field, while the writer's *Byzantine Art* (Penguin Books, 1954) is the most convenient cheaper work in English; references to its plates are given from time to time in brackets in the text, because it is easily accessible; there is a full series of plates of mosaics of all periods in W. Weidlé's *Mosaïques Palaechrétiennes et Byzantines* (Milan-Florence, 1954).

The author would like to express his thanks to Miss B. Morton of Edinburgh University for giving much time and care to typing the text; to Mrs. Margaret Scott for her careful work on drawings for the text figures; to Mr. R. Hoddinott of London and Mr. Ljubinković and Professor Radojčic of Belgrade for permitting him to use some of their photographs of Yugoslav paintings, and to Professor E. Dyggve, to Dr. Otto Demus, to the Byzantine Institute of America, and to various others who have provided photographs. He is indebted for more than he can say to those numerous scholars whose writings have provided information or inspired ideas—except in so far as these men are mentioned in the footnotes, they must remain anonymous.

Little more need be said. The tale is an enthralling one, concerned with a profoundly important aspect of the art and thought of the civilised world. As a whole it is not very familiar. The author's chief hope is that this book may serve to stimulate the interest of many who have hitherto known but little of it.

EDINBURGH, *July* 1957.

CONTENTS

Part V

LATER BYZANTINE ART

COLOUR PLATES

ILLUSTRATIONS *Following page*

LINE ILLUSTRATIONS

For map showing the principal centres and
other places mentioned in the text, *see endpapers*.

Part I

THE FOUNDATIONS

No art is born suddenly out of nothing; continuity has always been an essential of every phase, and it was especially important in early Christian art. All the regions of the nearer East where Christianity was first preached and practised had something to give, and there has been a good deal of argument as to which of them—Rome, the Hellenistic world, the east Mediterranean lands that were under Iranian influence— exercised the principal role. This argument, which has often in the past been coloured by a definite partisanship, is not taken up again here. Instead an attempt is made to show what was actually the legacy of each region, and how it was taken over and developed in the service of the Christian faith. Three primary styles have been distinguished, but this has involved a good deal of simplification, for the area concerned was large, the races inhabiting it were diverse and the cultures that they favoured were far from uniform. But though in a detailed study greater precision would be necessary, the three styles discussed in the following pages were un- doubtedly those that were most important in the first centuries of Christian art.

B

CHAPTER I

THE PICTURESQUE STYLE

A VERY great deal has been written about the respective roles of different sections of the pagan world in the establishment and formation of Christian art, and the authorities have argued—and still argue—as to which region played the most important part. Some have taken up the cudgels in favour of Rome, asserting that early Christian art was little more than a development of the pagan art of Italy. Others have urged the claims of the eastern Mediterranean, assigning the main initiative to Syria and Palestine, where, they assert, new ideas were developed in art which penetrated to other areas along with the new faith which was itself first practised in that area. Others assign a vital role to Asia Minor, where St. Paul preached and where the majority of the early "Fathers of the Church" had their homes and taught their followers. Others have set out the claims of Mesopotamia and Persia, where art of character and quality had been developed in the service of the Persian court and its minor satraps, or of faiths like Mithraism, to which Christianity, in its developed form, owed a certain debt. Or again a case has been put forward in favour of the aniconic character of the earliest Christian teaching, and it has been suggested that it was not until quite well on in the Christian age that a truly Christian art was first developed.[1]

In spite of arguments and counter-arguments, in spite of the assemblage of a great deal of evidence, and in spite of the very valuable researches conducted by scholars in the last half-century, however, the case is in reality rather more obvious than it might seem at first sight. The truth lies between, rather than along, the direct lines of any of these arguments. Each region, as it became Christianised, sought to adapt the art of which it was possessed to Christian usage, according to its own lights, and as contacts with other regions were developed and

[1] N. H. Baynes, "Idolatry and the Early Church", in *Byzantine Studies and other Essays*, London, 1955, pp. 116 ff., and especially p. 123.

as interchange of ideas took place, so artistic elements inter-
mingled also, so that local arts changed and developed, thanks
to the fresh influences that were introduced from outside. It
stands to reason, however, that areas where art was most
advanced naturally had the most to give, and that it was in
places where the new thought was most active that the most
progressive and profound developments took place. It is our
object, then, not so much to argue the claims of any one region
as against those of another, as to analyse the styles, and to show
by examination what it was that each style had to give. How
each legacy was in fact developed, and how it blended with
those of other styles, will, it is hoped, appear as the story is
outlined in the pages that follow.

It is, however, no easy matter to decide whether one should
begin a study of early Christian art by mentioning the name of
the Hellenistic or that of the Latin world, and cite first the city
of Alexandria or that of Rome. Both were of the first importance
in the development of art in late pagan times, and both
exercised an extensive influence on early Christendom. But as
one looks back from a viewpoint established in the tenth or
eleventh century—the golden age of early mediaeval art—the
debt owed to the Hellenistic world seems perhaps the more
considerable. And on that assumption it is to Alexandria that
we must first direct our attention.

Alexandria was a city of great wealth and of considerable
influence not only in the political and the economic spheres
but also in that of culture. It was the home of the greatest
library in the world, which had been established by Ptolemy II
Philadelphus (285-245 B.C.); it was the centre of neo-Platonic
studies, which played a leading role in pagan thought in the
early years of the Christian era, and also influenced the development of Christian ideology more or less unremittingly till the
last phase of Byzantine culture in the fifteenth century; and it
has been held that it was also the source of a very vital and
distinctive style in art which developed there shortly before the
beginning of the Christian era and which was characterised by
a three-dimensional, pseudo-realist outlook, by a love of
picturesque scenes and by a tendency to idealise both theme
and personality. This art is usually known as the "picturesque"
style.

Unfortunately we know very little of this art at first hand, for the ancient city of Alexandria lies buried below the modern one, and there has been very little attempt or even opportunity to excavate it. Except for a few sculptures and some copies of wall paintings now perished, that were discovered in a catacomb in the mid nineteenth century, there are practically no records of this art that survive. Indeed, their paucity tends to suggest that perhaps not quite as much work was actually done at Alexandria as some authorities would have us believe, for elsewhere, notably at Rome and Constantinople, casual finds have been far more numerous. Thus, though the "picturesque" style in early art is a fact which can be attested by numerous examples found elsewhere, it is really only on a theoretical basis that the origin and development of the style can be assigned to Alexandria. The numerous portraits from mummy cases of the Hellenistic period from Egypt as a whole, on the other hand, show that a great deal of work in another style, the "expressionist", was done there beyond question. This will be discussed in the second chapter.

The importance of Rome in the story of early art—or rather of the Roman world as a whole—is on the other hand attested by evidence of a more concrete character. A very considerable number of early paintings has survived in or near Rome itself, notably at Boscoreale, and there is a whole mass of material of the greatest wealth and importance from the shops, houses and villas of Pompeii and Herculaneum near Naples which can be exactly classified and dated, for the whole area was engulfed by the famous eruption of Vesuvius in A.D. 79, and the houses, their paintings and contents have been admirably preserved ever since, so that it is possible to appreciate the style and colouring of the paintings to an extent impossible elsewhere. But though it is there that the richest collection is to be seen to-day, it must not be forgotten that the preservation of these paintings is fortuitous, and that others equally rich and varied no doubt existed in other places.

Not all of this art of the Pompeian area belongs to the so-called "picturesque" style. Indeed, a great deal of what survives, in any case from the earlier houses at Pompeii, reproduces the true Hellenic art of ancient Greece in a very pure form, just as the sculptures which the Romans executed and admired more often than not reproduced Greek originals. Some of the paintings were indeed actually done by Greeks, and bear inscriptions in the Greek language; they show scenes from Greek literature or the figures of Greek mythology, and it is on the basis of such paintings that we can reconstruct our ideas of what was being done in ancient Greece itself in the fifth century B.C. A painting of Andromeda at Naples which follows very closely a Greek original of the fourth century B.C., by a Greek painter called Nikias, may serve as an example (Maiuri, pl. 1, p. 79). But these essentially classical paintings fall outside the scope of our subject, and it is the later ones at Pompeii, those done after about 100 B.C., that concern us, for the truly Hellenic works exercised but little influence in the formation of Christian art. Later, however, the influence of the Hellenic manner did have a part to play, and the resulting style may be distinguished by the term "neo-attic".

The very penetrating analyses of these paintings that have been undertaken by a whole series of scholars show them to have been inspired by two very distinct lines of thought, the one picturesque and poetic, the other more factual and prosaic; the former may be regarded as typical of a Greek, the latter of a Latin outlook. The presence of certain essentially Egyptian elements—animals, ornamental motifs and so on—in works of the former type, led the authorities to associate their origin with Alexandria. At some time shortly before the beginning of the Christian era the two styles were blended, light effects began to be studied for their own sake, and a new interest began to be taken in actual surroundings, so that there grew into being, for the first time in history, an art of pure landscape painting. A great many of the paintings that have survived at Pompeii belong to this category, though the degree of naturalism in the rendering of the landscape varies very considerably. Sometimes there are scenes which would appear to represent an actual landscape, seeming to be done almost with the easel out of doors; at other times the landscapes are obviously studio pieces; at other times again the natural landscape itself has ceased to play an important part in the picture, and instead the architectural elements which always featured in the landscapes are stressed, till the picture becomes what one may best term an architecturescape rather than a landscape. In this way there developed what was really a panoramic style, where architectural compositions rather like continuous panoramas were used as backgrounds for a number of separate

scenes enacted before them. These backgrounds remained extra-
ordinarily popular for many centuries to come; indeed they
continued to play an important role till the very last phases of
mediaeval Christian painting.

A number of attempts have been made to classify the paintings of Pompeii on the basis of the development of these
architectural motifs; the most notable of them is that which
was propounded by Mau in the last quarter of the last century.
He distinguishes four basic manners. The first is in the main
a landscape one, the landscapes being treated in an illusionistic
manner. This landscape style, with its poetic outlook and
imaginative conception, is really more Greek than Latin, for
the elements that must be regarded as characteristically Latin—
narrative content, exactitude of representation, lack of fantasy
—are absent. Accompanying the landscapes, and showing a
similar love of illusion yet rather closer observation of nature,
are the still lives, which, though they hardly concern us here,
nevertheless in themselves alone serve to attest the very great
qualities of Pompeian painting from an aesthetic point of view.

In Mau's second style architecture had become more important than landscape, but as the style developed, the fantastic
element was intensified, till eventually an interest in decoration
for its own sake superseded the original interest in representation almost completely. This progress towards a more imaginative outlook followed two distinct trends, the first exemplified
by a love of vistas, like those which we see developed in the
famous paintings of Boscoreale, the second characterised by a
love of linear decoration on a flat surface, which was more to
the fore at Pompeii. The latter style is often known as the
tapestry style. It became especially popular after about 50 B.C.,
and was characterised by a very lovely sense of colour. The
compositions are often to be described almost as dream
fantasies.

In Mau's third style architectural compositions gave place
almost entirely to motifs of a purely ornamental character, such
as candelabra, scrolls and so on. Vitruvius, writing between 40
and 28 B.C., refers to this change, and it seems to have reached
its full stage of development by about 20 B.C., even though the
old architectural style was not completely forgotten till well
into the Christian era. Indeed, art at this time had its advanced
and its conservative trends just as it has to-day, and it is not

always possible to date all its manifestations on the basis of
stylistic development alone. This is especially the case when an
attempt is made to distinguish Mau's fourth from his third
style, for the two certainly overlapped very considerably. Yet
the fourth style, in its developed form, is distinctive enough, for
a frail architectural framework of a rather baroque character
became dominant, and the framework was often shown against
a continuous white ground. The Casa di Sirico or the Casa dei
Vettii at Pompeii, both of around A.D. 50, are typical (Rizzo,
pls. XXI-XXIII).

Since Mau first embarked on a study of Pompeian art in the
eighties of the last century, there have been numerous new
discoveries and our knowledge and understanding have progressed very considerably, so that a number of new and more
detailed systems of classification have been suggested, especially
with regard to the "picturesque" style proper. One of these
again takes note of four styles (Maiuri, p. 38). The earliest is
called the "Encrustation" style, and comprises work of an
essentially decorative character akin to marble revetment; it
was in considerable favour until about 80 B.C. It was succeeded
by the "Perspective" style, in greatest favour from 80 to c. 10
B.C.; this corresponds to Mau's second style. The third manner,
which evolved directly from the second, shows a greater love of
decoration for its own sake, a new feeling for fantasy, and a
particularly effective use of colour. This phase, which was in
vogue from about 10 B.C. to A.D. 50, is usually called the
"Ornate", and it corresponds to some extent to Mau's third
group. The next style is called the "Intricate", and it corresponds exactly to Mau's fourth group.[1] It is surprising how
closely some of the paintings in this manner approximate to
the stage sets of such seventeenth century artists as the Bibiena.

Very shortly before the destruction of Pompeii, the custom
of enclosing views or other pictures inside a sort of wicker-
work frame became very popular. This framework usually
supported a platform of arabesques and tendrils. By the
second century this type of framing had become the dominant
one in other places than Pompeii, and it remained important
till Christian themes usurped the old classical ones.

---

[1] For a discussion of Mau's classification and for notes on later developments
see R. Hinks, *Catalogue of Greek, Etruscan and Roman Paintings and Mosaics in the
British Museum*, London, 1933.

All these styles exercised some influence on the development of Christian art, though in some cases it was greater than others. The architectural backgrounds which became popular in Byzantine manuscripts and wall paintings at the time of Justinian and remained so right down to the sixteenth century were thus derived from Pompeian or similar prototypes. Some of the great mosaic decorations, more especially those of St. George at Salonica and the Great Mosque at Damascus, consist of little else than variations on the architecturescape theme (Pl. 16). Looped up curtains which frequently accompanied the architectural compositions were very popular in the latest phases of pagan wall painting and were reproduced in later mosaics, wall paintings, manuscripts or even on ivories; they became particularly popular in the Carolingian world and in later Byzantine painting. The still lives which appear as enchanting details in many Byzantine decorations find their prototypes in the very lovely and finely conceived still life compositions of Pompeii. The technique, colouring and style of these pagan works left an obvious heritage in a great deal of Christian painting. But more important even than all this was the way in which actual figures and compositions were taken over from pagan art into the service of Christianity and developed as part of an entirely new iconography which remained in vogue until it was finally supplanted by Renaissance schemes in Italy and Gothic ones north of the Alps.

The immensity of the debt of early Christian art to the pagan world is nowhere better illustrated than in the paintings of the Catacombs around Rome, where are to be found the majority of the earliest of the truly Christian paintings that have come down to us. Unlike the paintings of Boscoreale, which were done for rich, prosperous and sophisticated patrons, however, the paintings of the Catacombs as a whole reflect the tastes of a very different society. Most Christians in early times were poor men and could not afford to sponsor expensive decorations or employ noted artists. But all, rich and poor alike, were moved by new ideas and a new outlook. They were not interested in elegant figures, delightful compositions or lovely decorations, but in the faith which they had adopted and which they sought to serve. Pure decoration thus tended to give place to illustration, usually of a dogmatic or narrative character, while elegance gave way to expression. But even so, there was still a good deal of decoration in the Catacombs, and these decorations, with scrolls, birds and so forth, were developed directly from pagan work. Moreover, the illustrations of Bible themes which as time went on became more and more important had to be evolved from what was already there; they were not suddenly created out of nothing, but were developed by the re-arrangement and re-interpretation of old pagan themes.

The debt to the ancient world is clear enough when we look at such paintings as those of the third century in the Catacomb of Praetextatus, where scrolls and birds form a principal part of the decoration. The birds show a real understanding and appreciation of nature, even if they are posed rather formally on either side of a vase; the scrolls are naturalistic at basis, even if arranged formally. The naturalism of their depiction attests the classical heritage; their formal posing belongs to the new age, for in many cases these naturalistic motifs had a symbolical significance. The motif of a vase between two adoring birds or animals thus properly belonged to an old eastern conception where the central motif represented the "hom", or tree of life, adored and revered by nature. In Christian art it symbolised the eucharist, and was taken over along with many another piece of ancient symbolism and was used by Christian artists for many centuries to come. Similarly the peacock assumed a new significance, for it symbolised the Resurrection, because its flesh was supposed to be incorruptible, while the fish was even more sacred, as the letters of its name in Greek ($IX\ThetaY\Sigma$) stood as an anagram for the words Jesus Christ, Son of God, Saviour ('$I\eta\sigma o\hat{v}s$ $X\rho\iota\sigma\tau\grave{o}s$ $\Theta\epsilon o\hat{v}$ $Y\grave{\iota}os$ $\Sigma\omega\tau\acute{\eta}\rho$).

Late third century work in the Catacomb of Domitilla again attests the influence of the "picturesque" style, notably in the scene of the Good Shepherd (Pl. 1). Our Lord is shown before a landscape background in which there are trees and animals; it still retains many of the attributes of the landscapes of Pompeii. Christ Himself is also still a figure of essentially classical character, and would hardly have seemed out of place in a pagan scene. In fact, the theme is Christian, but the rendering still shows clearly the style, even the iconography, of pagan art. Numerous similar pictures can be cited not only in the Catacombs but also among the sculptured sarcophagi or in the early mosaics of the Roman world. The period during which this style continued to retain an influence was quite long drawn out, and hints of the old style appear as late as the ninth or tenth century. It must suffice to compare the rendering of the Good Shepherd in the mosaics of Galla Placidia at Ravenna (*c*. 440); they show clearly enough the nature of this survival (Pl. 10).

But though most of the figures and many of the themes among the paintings of the Catacombs are still strikingly pagan, new influences had begun to penetrate and new ideas to develop well before the adoption of Christianity as the official religion, and the speed with which the new Christian iconography was formulated is perhaps even more remarkable than the way in which old ideas were retained. As early perhaps as the third century in the Catacomb of Priscilla we see the Virgin depicted as a figure illustrating a prophecy of Isaiah vii. 14 ("Behold, a virgin shall conceive, and bear a son, and shall call his name Immanuel") (Pl. 2, *a*). In that of Callixtus a whole series of scenes are shown, including the Woman of Samaria and the Last Supper, which are probably only slightly later in date. A rendering of the Virgin in the Coemeterium of Maius, of the fourth century, is however in quite a distinct style, which seems to illustrate the penetration of the more expressive eastern manner which will be discussed more fully in the next chapter (Pl. 3, *b*).

A course of evolution very similar to that which took place in the Catacombs of Rome was probably also enacted at Alexandria, though unfortunately there is no concrete evidence on which to build up a picture of its progress. Ptolemy Philadelphus had assembled seventy men there to translate the Old Testament from Hebrew to Greek—the version was that known as the Septuagint—and though the work was not completed till the second century A.D., it would seem that the text began to be illustrated at an early date, perhaps even before the Christian era. The discovery of a synagogue at Dura in Syria containing a series of wall paintings dating from about A.D. 245 serves to show that the Jews in early times did not eschew illustrations of the Old Testament as they do in their synagogues to-day (Pl. 3, *a*). Indeed, figural art seems to have been important among the Jews at the outset of the Christian era, even if it was afterwards forsaken.

None of the original illustrations of the Alexandrine version of the Septuagint has survived, but there is reason to believe that certain later manuscripts follow them very closely. The most important of these is the Joshua Rotulus in the Vatican, which is probably to be dated to round about 700 (see p. 100 and Pl. 15, *b*). A Psalter now in Paris (Bib. Nat. Gr. 139; see Pl. 18) is also in a very "antique" style, and it too may reproduce elements of the original Septuagint illustrations. These and other similar manuscripts will be discussed later on; for the moment it must suffice to call attention to the very classical character of the figures in the former and of the compositions, as well as the figures, in the latter.

But there are certain other works of the first centuries of Christianity that are also probably to be assigned to Alexandria which are in a less "picturesque" style, and which savour more of the manner we shall discuss in a subsequent chapter which is best termed the "neo-Attic", and one can only conclude that the styles were mingled at Alexandria just as they were at Pompeii. But at Alexandria the prosaic element which we defined above as the Latin was, so far as we can tell, absent.

Three distinct manners can thus be distinguished up to this point. Firstly there was the "picturesque" style, characterised by its love of landscape and imaginative architectural decoration; it was most fully developed at Pompeii, but no doubt existed at Alexandria also, though no examples have come down to us. Secondly there was the prosaic or narrative style, which may be regarded as the most typical Latin or Roman contribution, and which ¡played an important part when the time came to develop a Christian dogmatic art. And thirdly there was the more purely classical or "neo-Attic" style, marked by the polish and excellence of its workmanship, which penetrated to the Roman world through the copying of Greek works and which was also important at Alexandria. Indeed, some authorities, with C. R. Morey foremost among them, attribute to Alexandria the majority of the works in this style that have come down to us from the fourth century. Some were no doubt made there. But there were other important cities, more especially Antioch, which were also centres of art production, and from the day of its establishment as the capital of the Christian world in 330 Constantinople probably became more important than any of them. As we shall attempt to show in a subsequent chapter, it was there above anywhere else that the "neo-Attic" style was most in favour. Before passing on to a discussion of that manner and of the role of Constantinople, however, it will be best to dispose of the eastern Mediterranean, of Syria and Palestine, where was centred and developed another distinct manner, in which classical elements played a much less important part than at Pompeii or Alexandria. That style we have termed the "expressionist".

BOOKS

A. Maiuri, *Roman Painting*, Skira, 1953.

A. Mau, *Geschichte der dekorativen Wandmalerei in Pompeij*, Berlin, 1882.

G. E. Rizzo, *La Pittura Ellenistico-Romana*, Milan, 1929.

J. Wilpert, *Le pitture delle catacombe Romane*, Rome, 1903—there is also a German edition of this book.

CHAPTER II

THE EXPRESSIONIST STYLE

NOT all the paintings of Pompeii and other places in the Graeco-Roman world even in pagan times were in the "picturesque" manner or showed close affinity with the classical style. There are many works in which idealism and illusion are absent and where elegance, charm or concern with the direct narrative have given place to a distinct approach, characterised by a somewhat crude vigour, and where forcefulness replaces delicacy. A portrayal of the Virgin in the Coemeterium of Maius may be cited as an example of this approach in the heart of the Roman world (Pl. 3, *b*); numerous other examples could be named in Syria or Egypt. Here neither the elegance of Hellenism nor the factual narrative manner of Roman art are dominant. The approach is more emotional, more violent, and can perhaps best be described by borrowing a term that has become current in recent art criticism, namely "expressionist". In works of this type the artist's aim seems to have been to render above anything else the feeling or inner import of his subject, and as often as not beauty and charm were sacrificed and fine details omitted in so doing. Such works thus tend to lack delicacy and the more obvious elements of attraction, but they are instead effective, impressive and, often enough, of a very profound character. Art of this type was nothing new; the sculpture of ancient Mesopotamia, for example, was in essentially the same style, and a search after emotion and expression characterised the art of Asia Minor in Hellenistic times. But the outlook was foreign to Greece proper and also to the Roman world before the Christian era.

This change of outlook was accompanied by a number of technical and stylistic factors, notably the depiction of figures in rigid, frontal poses, an excessive enlargement of the heads in proportion to the rest of the body, and a rather careless treatment of the bodies themselves, which often tended to become ill-proportioned and dumpy. In sculpture, artists seemed to delight in a rather rough finish, as opposed to the immaculate polish and smoothness of the best Greek work, and they liked to use the drill rather than the chisel, thereby achieving deep contrasting relief rather than a smooth, attractive surface. In painting, the subtle gradation of tones, so characteristic of the "picturesque" style, was avoided, and instead harsh, rather brilliant colours were used, in strange but often effective juxtaposition.

Perhaps the most striking examples of this style in the Roman world are afforded by a number of statues in porphyry of the fourth century, notably two in the Vatican and two representing Tetrarchs, which are built into the south-western corner of St. Mark's at Venice (Fig. 1). But there are a few figures among the paintings of Pompeii which suggest that the same manner was known to painters working there very early in the Christian era, and there are others among the Catacomb paintings which quite definitely also belong to this trend.

E. H. Swift, in a recent book, has suggested that such works as these represent nothing more than a decadence of Roman art,[1] and it is quite true that a good deal of very clumsy work was produced in the Roman world which can be accounted for in this way. But even so, there can be little doubt but that the "expressionist" style as a whole represented something much more definite than mere decadence. Rostovtzev has shown that frontality is to be associated with a definite style in art which perhaps had its birth in the Syro-Hittite world, though it was much developed and probably also disseminated by the Parthians,[2] and recent discoveries and investigations in Syria furnish valuable evidence as to the evolution of the style as a whole and of the way in which it came into being.

The earliest monuments that show the style in a fully developed state would appear to belong to the first century of the Christian era and are represented to-day by the paintings of the famous Temple of the Palmyrene gods at Dura, on the upper Euphrates, dating from A.D. 85, as well as by tomb paintings and sculptures at Palmyra. In all these works the figures are rigid and assume severely frontal positions; the rendering is two rather than three dimensional, and where paintings are concerned the colouring is brilliant and effective,

---

[1] *Roman Sources of Christian Art*, New York, 1951, *passim*.
[2] "Dura and the Problem of Parthian Art", *Yale Classical Studies*, V, 1935, p. 238.

FIG. 1.   Stone sculpture.   Two Tetrarchs.   *c.* 300.
St. Mark's, Venice.

but lacks the half-tones and subtlety of the "picturesque" style. At a later date, when the "expressionist" style was fully developed, a more exuberant, florid manner came to the fore in place of the rather precise, svelte approach which dominated at Palmyra. This more developed "expressionist" style is exemplified by certain rather later works at Dura, notably some of the wall paintings in a synagogue and in a small church, both of which date from about A.D. 245 (Pl. 3, *a*). The paintings in both are closely akin, and if not by the same hand, were in any case from the same workshop. Their preservation was to a great extent due to the fact that both buildings were buried more or less in entirety in the process of reinforcing the city wall.

Here the contrasting colours and the frontal attitudes characteristic of the earlier paintings in the Temple of the Palmyrene gods reappear, but the very formal treatment of the earlier work gives place to what is at the same time a more florid but also a more primitive approach, which is probably to be attributed to the fact that the church and the synagogue were small and the patrons poor, whereas the Temple of the Palmyrene gods was a major monument, done by an artist of great skill. The story that the paintings record also begins to play a more vital part than in the earlier work, and the scenes are not only of an essentially narrative character but also more dynamic, in that they tell a tale which develops and unfolds, whereas the scene in the Temple of the Palmyrene gods is a purely static one. What is particularly important, however, is the fact that both in the synagogue and in the church the iconography of a whole number of scenes of the Old Testament story already appears in a fully developed form. No doubt the scenes were based on illustrations to the Septuagint, which had been conceived soon after its translation at Alexandria, but even so, it is significant to find these fully developed themes in the East at much the same date that they were also being worked out in the Catacombs of Rome. The results, though similar, were not always the same, and it thus seems that there must have been a separate eastern iconography as well as a separate eastern style in Christian art and that this was developed before the middle of the third century A.D.

Unfortunately the Dura paintings stand to-day very much alone. They should not, however, be regarded as isolated monuments. There must have been numerous paintings in the same style and of the same type in synagogues and in small churches all over Syria and Palestine before about 330, and the style must have continued in favour in the decoration of the larger churches which were built under the patronage of Constantine and his successors after the adoption of Christianity as the

Fig. 2.   Lead ampulla from Monza.
Sixth century.

official religion of the state. But of these larger works, all of which have perished, we can build up no more than a very vague picture, based on the paintings of the smaller churches, on a few contemporary descriptions, and on certain small-scale minor works like the Monza ampullae which, for archaeo-logical reasons, must date from before 614. These take the form of small flat flasks, which were used by pilgrims for carrying holy oil; they are decorated on their two main faces with figures often in the orans position (Fig. 2). They tell us nothing of the iconography of the scenes, but do show that single figures or small groups, often with arms raised in prayer, were much in favour in the eastern world at the time.

Rather more comprehensive evidence is afforded by the depiction of a number of actual scenes which appear on the lid of a little wooden reliquary in the Vatican (Pl. 11). They include the Marys at the Tomb, the Ascension, the Crucifixion, the Nativity and the Baptism. The reliquary must date from the sixth century. The work is obviously related to the Dura paintings in style, and the iconography is characteristically eastern, as for example in the long robe worn by Christ in the Crucifixion scene, in place of the loin cloth usual in the Byzantine world and the West. Eastern again is the arrangement of the Annunciation, where the angel comes from the right; in the western world she approaches from the left. The movement of scenes seems to follow that of writing; in the West it is from left to right, in the East from right to left, as is the case with the Syriac script. Other examples of the work of the eastern school are provided by the illuminations of a manuscript now in the Laurentian library at Florence, which was written by a monk of the name of Rabula at Zagba in upper Mesopotamia in 586. In addition to the Crucifixion, where the Christ wears the same long robe, the manuscript contains four other full-page illustrations, the finest of which depicts the Ascension, and there are also a number of scenes on a smaller scale. The colouring is rich and brilliant and the iconography fully developed.

Such other works of Syrian origin as are to be assigned to the fifth or sixth century mostly take the form of ivory carvings. Most important of them is one in the British Museum bearing the Adoration above and the Nativity below (Fig. 3). The severely frontal Virgin, the large heads and awkward movements are typical of the school, as is the use of a hole done with a drill to represent the pupil of the eye. It is possible that originally some sort of precious stone was fixed into this hole; such "colourful" treatment would have been in full accord with the oriental character of the school. Typical again is the way in which the size of the principal figure in each scene is enlarged

FIG. 3. Ivory: the Adoration and Nativity. Syria or Palestine.
Sixth century. British Museum,

in proportion to the others, an idea which once again belongs to the East and is foreign to the Greek world. It is only necessary to contrast a Greek sculpture or Greek myth, where gods and men appear as equals, with an Egyptian or a Mesopotamian one, where kings and gods are a race apart. There is a very similar ivory in the John Rylands library at Manchester which belongs to the same date and probably came from the same workshop.

Many of these works are no doubt primitive, having been done for tiny chapels or poor patrons. But the argument put forward by certain critics that their nature and character is merely the result of their poverty cannot be regarded as valid, for in the first place works in different materials, produced in different places and at different epochs, are all in the same manner, and in the second place it is possible to discover not only a distinctive eastern iconography but also a definite style running through the work, and this is parallel to a trend which dominated eastern thought at the time, and which finds its origin in the teaching and outlook of the "Fathers of the Church". In fact, the art is a Christian art, produced consciously in the service of Christianity as it was conceived by these men, and the artists responsible for these works were striving after a definite object even if they did not always fully succeed in achieving their aims.

As time went on, the Syrian style became more distinctive. The large heads and expressive rather dumpy figures thus tended to become further exaggerated, and scrollwork became heavy and florid; progressive stress was also laid upon the inner meaning of the themes. Perhaps the most important examples of this more advanced Syrian style are a silver plaque in the Louvre bearing a stylite on his column, which must belong to the fifth century, and two patens, one in the Museum of Antiquities at Constantinople and the other in the Woods Bliss collection at Washington, which are to be dated late in the sixth or early in the seventh century (*Byzantine Art*, pl. 55, *a*). Both depict the Communion of the Apostles, with Christ shown twice on each plate in the guise of a priest, once giving the Bread and once the Wine. They are both in a wholly east Mediterranean style.

Certain other pieces of silver are rather less primitive, and bear scrolls and figures which are basically classical, though they are still eastern rather than western. Most important of them is a chalice, now in New York, which must date from soon after 400. It is usually known as the Antioch chalice, for it was found not far from that city and was quite possibly made there. There is reason to believe that Antioch was important as a centre of metal working and ivory carving at the time, and it is probable that much of the work done there was in the more classical manner of the chalice rather than the more primitive one of the British Museum and Manchester ivories, for it was a rich city with a cultured population, and certainly a great many of the mass of mosaic pavements which have recently been unearthed there were of a very sophisticated character, and in the "picturesque" or "neo-Attic" rather than the "expressionist" style.

These floors extend in date from the first to the sixth century; there is nothing later, for the city was virtually destroyed by an earthquake in 526 and it never really recovered. All are of a secular character, and there is nothing from Antioch on a large scale that betokens that the patrons were Christians. Perhaps, as in Rome, the richer classes were conservative and mostly still pagan. The pavements of the second, third and even fourth centuries are extremely accomplished and show a mingling of the "picturesque" and "neo-Attic" styles in almost equal degrees. Only with the fifth century did oriental elements begin to penetrate; then not only did the style change but the iconography also, and hunting scenes and animal combats of a distinctly Persian type began to dominate the repertory in place of the old classical motifs. These themes travelled farther afield than Antioch, for we find them widely disseminated, notably in Constantinople, in Rome, in Sicily and even in North Africa. They remained popular in any case till the middle of the sixth century, but after that time themes of a secular character tended to become less important.

The examples of the "expressionist" style which we have cited so far all belong to Syrian soil and the role of Syria in the development of this style was considerable.[1] But works in the same manner were produced elsewhere, notably in what is to-day Asia Minor, and Morey goes so far as to suggest that the style actually originated there and not in Syria.[2] He thus sees the

[1] G. de Francovich, "L'arte siriaca e il suo influsso", in *Commentari*, II, p. 8.
[2] *Art Bulletin*, VII, 1921.

style in embryo in the great frieze at Pergamon of the third century B.C. The vibrant dynamic quality of the work is perhaps its outstanding characteristic, but there is also a great love of the pathetic, and, more important, it was at Pergamon that the element of pain first entered into art, for example in such a sculpture as the well-known "Dying Gaul" in the Capitoline Museum at Rome. It was this stress of unpleasant emotional factors, he thinks, that led to the development of "expressionism" in art. It is certainly true that from the time of the carving of the Pergamon altar the "expressionist" outlook became very important in Asia Minor, and it is very probable that it penetrated even in pagan times into Syria, where it became mingled with influences from Mesopotamia and Persia. It is not surprising to find that the development of such an outlook was spurred on by Christianity, which was, after all, profoundly concerned with the expression of what may be termed supra-normal emotions, and a preoccupation with these led on the one hand to an attempt to express transcendental themes in art, while on the other the idea of pain and suffering tended to become associated with that of holiness, as we see in the lives of the martyrs or anchorites, who believed that they could attain to a state of godliness by means of mortifying the flesh. Their outlook was very characteristic of that which dominated eastern Christianity, and with it eastern Christian art, at the time.

There is a great deal to be said for Morey's "Anatolian thesis", and there can be no doubt as to the importance of the role played by Asia Minor in the development of new artistic ideas. But we still have a great deal to learn about what Asia Minor stood for in art in the first five centuries of Christendom, and one day a very important book bringing up to date the tentative theories of Strzygowski, as set out in his *Asia Minor, a New Sphere of Art History*, will be written. But the time for it is not yet ripe. While surveys, excavations and studies relating to Syria, Italy, Greece and the Balkans have been pushed forward with the greatest energy since the beginning of the twentieth century, practically nothing has been done in Asia Minor, and our knowledge is still more or less at the stage it had reached when Strzygowski published his epoch-making work in 1903.

Not all that Strzygowski then said can be accepted as gospel; but just because a great deal of important new material has subsequently been found in Italy and none in Asia Minor, there are not adequate grounds for decrying all that he had to say with regard to the importance of the eastern Mediterranean, and indeed excavations that have recently been carried out on the site of the Great Palace of the Byzantine emperors at Constantinople and journeys and surveys that have been made in the last few years in Cilicia by Mr. Michael Gough have served to show that a great deal of what Strzygowski had to say regarding methods of construction in brickwork and as to the early date of churches in the East was not mere theoretical supposition, as his critics have so often maintained.[1]

Much of what Strzygowski had to say about Asia Minor had to do with architecture, and is therefore outside the scope of this book. Certain works of art in sculpture and painting that were produced in Asia Minor in the age of the formation of Christian art are on the other hand very much our concern. First may be noted a group of sarcophagi of which there are numerous examples; they must have been produced by a large school of sculptors, working in a particular region over a long period of time, so that the question of individual style is less important than that of regional and temporal taste. This school is usually known as the Lydian, and it was responsible for a group of sarcophagi often known, from the name of one of the most famous examples, as the Sidamara group, though actually the Sidamara ones constitute a sub-group within the larger Lydian one. All the sarcophagi bear full-length figures on the sides and at the ends, arranged against architectural back-grounds, not dissimilar from those so popular in the Pompeian paintings. The earlier examples are to be dated to the second, the later to the third, fourth or even the early fifth century. All are characterised by a rather profuse, fussy type of ornament, in the carving of which the drill was extensively used. In the

---

[1] The problems of construction will be fully discussed by Ward Perkins in the *Second report on excavations carried out on behalf of the Walker Trust of St. Andrews in the Great Palace of the Byzantine Emperors at Constantinople*, Edinburgh, 1958. In brief, they show that in the fifth and sixth centuries the method of construction in practice at Constantinople was that proper to the eastern world where vaults were built without centering by laying the bricks at an angle, and not that in favour at Rome, where the bricks were set vertically and had to be supported on a wooden centering while construction was in progress, or where masses of concrete were used on an extensive scale. Some of the results of exploration are noted by M. Gough, "Early Churches in Cilicia", in *Byzantinoslavica*, XVI, 1955, p. 201. See also his articles in *Anatolian Studies*, II, 1952, and IV, 1954.

Rome. Catacomb of Domitilla. The Good Shepherd. Third century. (*After Wilpert.*)

PLATE I

(b) Constantinople. Mosaic from the Great Palace: Mother and Child. c. 450. (Photo Walker Trust.)

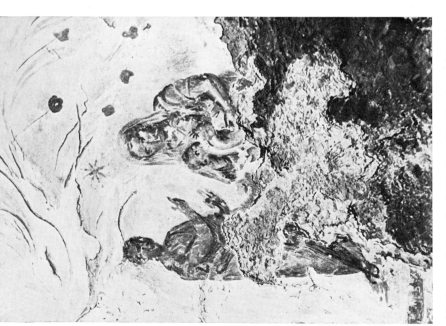

(a) Rome. Catacomb of Priscilla. The Prophecy of Isaiah. Early third century. (After Wilpert.)

(b) Rome. Coemeterium of Maius. Virgin and Child.
Fourth century. (*Photo Anderson.*)

PLATE 3

(a) Dura. The Synagogue. Moses and the Burning Bush.
c. 245. (*Damascus Museum.*)

Head of an Apostle from Ephesus. Late fourth century.
(*Photo Kunsthistorisches Museum, Vienna.*)

PLATE 4

later examples arcades replace the gables which are typical of
the architectural elements of the earlier ones, and the repertory
of figures is enlarged, the figures growing in size as well as in
profusion, at the expense of the architecture. With the fourth
century Christian figures replaced pagan ones, though iconographically the fact that they are Christian is not always easy
to distinguish. The Evangelists thus resemble pagan philo-
sophers, while our Lord takes on the character of a classical
divinity. He was usually shown with long hair and youthful
appearance, like an Apollo, till the fourth century, when a
more dignified bearded figure began to become popular,
inspired no doubt by the teaching of the Fathers of the Church
on the one hand and the ideas of an iconography which
penetrated from the Semitic arts of Mesopotamia on the other.

The most familiar example of the group is a fragmentary
sarcophagus now at Berlin dating from about 400, which shows
Christ long-haired but beardless, between two Apostles, enclosed in gabled niches (Fig. 4). The debt to classical art is
obvious so far as superficial form is concerned, but the large
heads, the frontal poses, and the formal treatment of the
architectural ornament are all characteristic of the "expressionist" or eastern approach.

More fully "expressionist" in outlook than these sarcophagi
is a head unearthed during the Austrian excavations at
Ephesus, and usually dated to the end of the fourth century
(Pl. 4). It is a work of very expressive character—indeed one
might describe it as the very epitome of the "expressionist"
style at this period. It probably represents an Apostle, and the
strangely pathetic yet sympathetic feeling that it inspires marks
it out as a work of real distinction; its sculptor was certainly a
master of great ability, and here one has to consider the work
of an individual rather than that of a workshop, as was the
case with the Sidamara sarcophagi. But though the head is
obviously to be singled out as a work of very personal character,
it was also probably one of the products of a school which was
seeking—and achieving—very definite and distinctive aims in
the way of transcendental "expressionism".

Unfortunately no paintings of early date on a large scale have
so far been discovered in Asia Minor, but there is reason to
believe that one of the few manuscripts of the age that has come
down to us, that known as the Sinope fragment in the Biblio-

FIG. 4. Sarcophagus from Sidamara, Asia Minor.
Sixth century. Berlin Museum.

thèque Nationale at Paris, was produced there.[1] Though the
figures are ill-proportioned, they are nevertheless expressive
and lively, the colours are brilliant and effective, and the
illuminations tell the stories with which they are concerned
vividly and forcefully.

[1] A. Grabar, *Les Peintures de l'Evangélaire de Sinope*, Paris, 1948.

Whether the "expressionist" style was first conceived in Asia Minor, as Morey suggests, or in Syria, it was mainly thanks to the influence of Syria that the style spread to other places, and nowhere was it more intensively developed than in Egypt. With the exception of Alexandria and its immediate neighbourhood, which remained faithful to classical styles and ideas longer probably than any other centre, Egypt was on the whole a fortress of the "expressionist" school, and practically all the work that was produced there under Christian patronage was of that character. The fine Hellenistic mummy portraits of the first and second centuries are characterised by the frontal positions, the bright, rather harsh colours, and the forceful expressions that go to distinguish this school; there is little of the illusionism or idealism about them that we noted as the attributes of Alexandrine work. And the earliest paintings done for Christian patrons in Egypt show the "expressionist" characteristics to just as developed a degree as the later ones. The most important of them are those at Baouit and Saqqara.[1] The former are clumsy as to proportions and rather harsh in colour, with a great predominance of yellow. They are nevertheless quite effective, even if they lack delicacy. Those at Saqqara show the same love of deep shade and brilliant light and the same rather coarse modelling that characterised Syrian work, yet at the same time there is a quite profound understanding of spiritual values.

A glance shows the affinities that bind these paintings to Syria. But local ideas and beliefs had an important part to play in the development of art in Egypt. A number of ancient Egyptian themes were taken over and adopted in the service of Christianity, and characteristically Christian-Egyptian themes were developed as a result. Certain saints thus took on an Egyptian appearance, and aspects of local religious teaching or prejudice were reflected in art. Thus in the inscriptions the Virgin is in Egypt designated as ἡ ἁγία Μαρία (St. Mary), whereas in the Byzantine world and even in Syria she was usually called Θεοτόκος or Μήτηρ Θεοῦ, that is Mother of God. The difference in outlook that this denotes is very considerable, and it was reflected in the nature of the art. Egyptian work thus

---

[1] Peirce and Tyler, *Art Byzantin*, II, pl. 37, *a*. For detailed publication of Baouit see Clédat, *Le Monastère et la nécropole de Baouit*; for Saqqara, Quibell, *Excavations at Saqqara*.

left less to the imagination than the true Byzantine and it tended to seek for less transcendental ends.

In addition to the wall paintings, one or two religious panels of early date have survived from Egypt; one of the most important, which represents Christ and a Saint, is now in the Louvre. Ochre, sepia, salmon-red and grey-blue are the predominant colours, and these bright but rather ill-assorted hues are typical. Work of this sort, though of ever-declining quality, continued to be produced even after the Islamic conquest of Egypt about 640. Some tenth century wall paintings at Deir es Suryani may be noted. Ivory or bone carvings characterised by an exuberance almost Indian were produced in quite large numbers. But it is probably the textiles that show later Egyptian or Coptic art at its best. The Egyptians had always been good weavers and embroiderers, both crafts being mainly in the hands of the Christians, and a great deal of work was done for export as well as for home consumption both before and after the Muslim conquest. The character of the decoration was thus less governed by local than by international tastes. But it is probable that the importance of the role that has been assigned to Egypt with regard to textile production in the past has often been exaggerated owing to the fact that, thanks to its dry climate, more material has survived on Egyptian soil than elsewhere. Had we as many actual stuffs in our museums to-day from the looms of Syria, Asia Minor or Constantinople as we have from those of Egypt, our views as to the respective importance of the various centres would probably be very different.

BOOKS

J. H. Breasted, *Oriental Forerunners of Byzantine Painting*, Chicago, 1924.

G. Duthuit, *La Sculpture copte*, Paris, 1931.

Doro Levi, *Antioch Mosaic Pavements*, Princeton, 1947.

C. R. Morey, *Mediaeval Art*, New York, 1942.

H. Peirce and R. Tyler, *Art Byzantin*. Vols. I and II only appeared; they cover the period from about 300 to 700.

CHAPTER III

THE NEO-ATTIC STYLE

THE third principal style which played an important part in the formation of Byzantine and indeed of all early Christian art is that which Morey has distinguished as the "neo-Attic". It had already developed as a distinctive manner in the last two centuries before Christ, and was characterised above anything else by its conservatism: a conservatism of Hellenic forms and ideas, unaffected by the picturesque manner of Alexandria and Pompeii on the one hand or by the more dramatic outlook of Syria and Asia Minor on the other. As is often the case with conservative styles, it tended to be rather cold, academic and unemotional, but, even at periods of decadence, works in the "neo-Attic" manner were distinguished by technical excellence, and in this respect they contrast very noticeably with the more clumsy, even if more spontaneous, products of Syria. Yet the style found nevertheless quite a happy home in the east Mediterranean, for though at variance with the more exaggerated aspects of the "expressionist" style, it had much in common with the two-dimensional, ornamental trend in art which had flourished in northern Mesopotamia in Assyrian times and which had left a heritage behind it which was to flourish anew under Islam. Morey even goes so far as to state that Antioch was one of the main centres of the "neo-Attic" style, and its influence is certainly to be seen in the ornamental sculptures at Baalbec and other Hellenistic cities in Syria of the second century A.D.

The style not only flourished in the eastern Mediterranean, however; it also penetrated to Rome, where it went far towards satisfying the tastes of the Roman plutocracy of the last century B.C. and the first three centuries of the Christian era. Such a monument as the famous Ara Pacis, set up for Augustus in 13 B.C., is thus essentially "neo-Attic" and affords evidence of the love of the more academic aspects of classical art that characterise the age. Numerous other sculptures in the same manner were executed in the centuries that followed, and the style was especially to the fore in the days of Hadrian, who was in every way of life an ardent pro-Athenian. Sharp outlines, crisp modelling, a love of frieze compositions and a habit of posing all the figures in the same plane against a blank background characterised the sculptures of the Hadrianic school. Thereafter similar work was especially favoured by the more conservative, and hence pagan, elements of the population, and no finer or more complete example of the style exists than the ivory diptych, now divided between the Victoria and Albert and the Cluny Museums, which bears the names of the Symmachi and the Nicommachi families (*Byzantine Art*, pl. 45). It is to be dated to about 400. The classical subject and the essentially conservative treatment are typical. The problem is to what centre should the work be assigned? Peirce and Tyler regard it as western; Morey singles it out as typical of the more conservative side of what was being done at Alexandria; Delbrueck and others have assigned it to Rome. In this case Rome seems most probable, for the ivory does not show the eclecticism which seems to have been characteristic of Constantinople at a rather later date, and the picturesque elements which it would seem were typical of Alexandria are also absent, as are all oriental or "expressionist" traits.

There is again nothing that is not really entirely Roman about the great sarcophagi of porphyry which were used for the burial of the earliest emperors at Constantinople and which have now mostly been collected in the court of the Museum of Antiquities there. Like the sarcophagus of Constantia now in the Vatican, they follow exactly the trend that one would expect a work done in the New Rome in a society which had adopted Christianity—that is to say, motifs like the Chi-Rho cross slowly supplanted the "inhabited" scrolls of the pagan world, and more abstract compositions gradually replaced the fully naturalistic ones. But the change only came about slowly. The sarcophagi were probably carved locally, for there is nothing the least Egyptian about them, though the material of which they were made must have been imported from Egypt, for it was not quarried elsewhere.

If the imperial sarcophagi of the early centuries of official Christianity were still essentially Roman, carvings in local materials showed a more rapid change of style, especially at

Constantinople. Happily quite a lot of material is available for study in the Museum of Antiquities there, thanks to discoveries made during the last forty or fifty years. Some of these have been purely fortuitous, owing to the digging of trenches for water mains or sewers which modern life has necessitated. Others have been produced by scientifically conducted excavations, like those done by the French in the Mangana area just after the first world war, those sponsored by the British Academy in the Hippodrome in 1927 and 1928, or those of the Walker Trust in a section of the Great Palace between 1935 and 1954. Sculptures of very fine quality have often turned up in quite minor excavations, not to mention a mass of other things, more especially pottery. A few especially important pieces among these sculptures may be mentioned.

Perhaps the most outstanding of them is a sarcophagus bearing Apostles at the ends and two angels supporting a Chi-Rho cross at the sides which must date from the fourth or early fifth century (Fig. 5). The sculpture is of a high technical excellence; the proportions of the figures are elegant and the rendering delicate. Though the subject matter is purely Christian, the spirit savours of Attic work of the fourth century B.C., and there is little here of the more florid Hellenistic approach, still less of the full-fledged "expressionist" style. The way in which the foliage is treated on a pedestal, also in the Istanbul museum, which was unearthed in 1927, shows a closely similar understanding, and if the sarcophagus serves to illustrate what is typically "neo-Attic" in figure sculpture around 500, the pedestal is equally typical of this style in non-representational ornament at the same date.[1] Like many another "neo-Attic" work, it heralds the style that was to become specifically Byzantine from the sixth century onwards.

Examples of the style in stone sculpture could be multiplied by citing other works in the Museum of Antiquities at Istanbul, but far more important are some of the figures in the great mosaic of the Imperial Palace unearthed at Constantinople on behalf of the Walker Trust of St. Andrews between 1935 and 1954. This mosaic is certainly one of the most important monuments of art of the late classical or early Byzantine age that has yet been discovered. It was, when it was complete, of an

---

[1] For the sarcophagus see Morey, *Early Christian Art*, fig. 102, and for the pedestal, Peirce and Tyler, II, pl. 42.

FIG. 5. Sarcophagus, Constantinople. Fifth century.
Museum of Antiquities, Istanbul.

immense extent, and all of it was technically of the very first excellence. Moreover, the figures and scenes, the trees and the formal patterns that constitute its decoration are all of great beauty, full of life and redolent of quality. The technical excellence of this mosaic is already a characteristic of the "neo-Attic" style; the conservatism of many of the extremely diverse motifs that compose the floor is equally so. This is particularly the case with regard to the human figures. Some of them, like that of a seated philosopher, are almost Athenian in their classic calm and sobriety. But even if they savour of an older art, some of these figures herald later, purely Christian developments like that of a mother nursing her child, which could have served as a prototype for a Christian composition of the Madonna (Pl. 2, b).

There are, however, other elements in the mosaic than those which are to be counted as primarily "neo-Attic", for the "neo-Attic" was not the only style at Constantinople. An enchanting water-mill thus savours of the "picturesque" style, as do the details of the landscapes, and some of the scenes like that showing shepherds milking their goats and sheep, or that with horses grazing or a man fishing, are again more "picturesque" than anything else. A great moustached head in the border, on the other hand, has about it something of the vigour of the "expressionist" style. But even so, in spite of this, and of the basically oriental character of the hunting scenes, the style is refined and elegant, the work fresh and brilliant, and the mosaic falls more happily into the "neo-Attic" than into any other group. But work in the "expressionist" manner was also done at Constantinople, in any case at a rather earlier date, and the sculptures of the famous base of Theodosios, set up in the Hippodrome about 390, savour of this style; the frontal positions of the figures and their large heads and staring eyes are indeed typical, though it is finer and more elaborate than is the general run of Syrian things (Fig. 6).

The more expressive style that we see here was, however, by the fifth century much less important at Constantinople than the more polished "neo-Attic", and in addition to the larger works found on the spot there are a number of things on a small scale which can for one reason or another also be assigned to the capital. The most important of them are some silver vessels which bear stamps or hall-marks on their bases, and

D

FIG. 6.   Base of the Obelisk of Theodosios, Constantinople. *c.* 390.

which can be dated and assigned to Constantinople, thanks to these. Most of them come from south Russia, where they were no doubt sent in early times as presents to keep the nomads of the region in a propitious mood. They were subsequently used as part of the burial furniture of nomad chieftains and they remained in the graves till excavated in recent times. Some of the most important come from a place called Concesti and are now in the Hermitage Museum at Leningrad. Other similar pieces have reached museums in western Europe and America. Nearly all are to be dated to the sixth or early seventh century, yet their designs are all very classical in subject and conservative in treatment, and at first glance one would be tempted to assign many of them to the same date as vessels from the Traprain or Mildenhall hoards in Britain, that is to say the third, fourth or early fifth century. The "neo-Attic" style is especially to the fore on an amphora from Perscepina or on a bowl in the Hermitage, bearing a shepherd watching his flocks[1]; the designs on both are of a very classical character. But the "neo-Attic" manner is also illustrated on a paten, known as the dish of Paternus, where the subject matter is limited to a cross, a small scroll and an inscription. It is dated to 518. It seems to illustrate the style in what is essentially a contemporary rather than a conservative vein. Another vessel, from Klimova, is stylistically very similar to the Barberini ivory (see p. 54), and like the ivory, is probably to be dated to the time of Anastasius; the hall-mark could apply equally well to that Emperor or to Justinian.

A dish in the Metropolitan Museum bearing David struggling with the lion is clearly another example of the same group, and must also have been made in Constantinople.[2] It is important, for the design is closely paralleled on a textile fragment now in the Cathedral treasury at Aachen and it has been suggested that the textile was made at the same place as the bowl.[3] There are references in the texts to the fact that Constantinople held a monopoly for the export of silks in the time of Justinian,[4] but

---

[1] Matszulewitsch, *Byzantinische Antike*, Berlin and Leipzig, 1929, pls. 28, 31. See also pl. 26, and p. 112.

[2] This is clear if it is compared with the vessels published by Matszulewitsch. Morey, however, believed it to be Alexandrine, "The Sources of Mediaeval Art", *Art Bulletin*, VII, 1924, p. 40.

[3] Peirce and Tyler were the first to point out this similarity, *Art Byzantin*, II, pl. 183.

[4] Procopios, *Anecdota*, XXV, 22. Loeb edition, London, 1935, Vol. VI, p. 300.

this is the first piece which can be attributed to the capital on factual evidence, even if the evidence is circumstantial rather than direct.

The attribution of textiles to particular centres is not easy, but it is likely that some should be assigned to Constantinople on the basis of the majesty, grandeur and excellence of their designs. Of such a character is the superb stuff in the Vatican bearing the Annunciation and Baptism in medallions (*Byzantine Art*, pl. 60), which in respect of colouring and technique is closely akin to the Aachen fragment. The only other locality in which it might have been made would seem to be Alexandria, where there were certainly important looms; it was indeed associated with that place by Von Falke.[1] But that identification seems unlikely, firstly on stylistic grounds, and secondly because no very similar stuffs have been found in graves in Egypt. Yet Egypt, thanks to its dry climate, is practically the only place in which textiles have been found in any quantity so-to-speak *in situ*, and one would expect to see included among the material from Egypt examples of all the types that were manufactured on the Egyptian looms.

Another outstanding piece of silver which is essentially of the "neo-Attic" group is a plate in the Museum of Antiquities at Istanbul bearing an elegant if rather severe figure seated frontally with animals and birds at the sides, which has been identified as a personification of India (Fig. 7). It is to be dated to the late fifth century. It was found at Lampsacus on the Black Sea and has, for no very clear reason, sometimes been attributed to Antioch. But the whole style savours of the capital, and with such major monuments as the mosaics of the Great Palace and the sculptures in the Istanbul museum before us, all of which were undoubtedly produced in Constantinople, an attribution to the capital in respect of the silver plate can hardly be disputed.

Work which shows a similar grandeur and elegance, even if the subject matter is not quite so classical, is to be found on some of the ivories of this age, and it may be suggested that many of these should be assigned to Constantinople rather than to one of the other centres where ivory carving was done. For

---

[1] *Kunstgeschichte der Seidenweberei*, Berlin, 1913, I, p. 50. The nature of the rosettes and other details of the ornament suggests a date in the seventh or eighth century rather than in the sixth, as Von Falke suggested.

FIG. 7. Silver dish, Constantinople. The Personification of India.
Sixth century. Museum of Antiquities, Istanbul.

one reason or another, however, each authority has tended in nearly every case to favour some other centre rather than the capital. Ivories have thus been assigned, somewhat indiscriminately at times, to Antioch, Rome or Alexandria; Milan has been favoured as a centre of production, and possibly Ravenna also; and a school of carving has even been localised in Provence. Though stylistic and historical evidence suggests that ivories were carved in all these places, it surely stands to reason that more work was done at the capital, Constantinople, than elsewhere, for it was there that the court was situated, there that ecclesiastical patronage had its centre, and there that the richer nobles congregated. Yet but few ivories have been attributed to the workshops there, apart from a number of Consular diptychs which can be assigned to the capital because of the inscriptions that they bear.

On the basis of evidence now available, nothing could be conceived as being more typical of all that Constantinople stood for in art than such an ivory as the famous Barberini diptych in the Louvre.[1] It is made up of several panels, the central one bearing a mounted Emperor, at one time believed to be Constantine and at another Justinian, but now identified as Anastasius because of the similarity of the face to that on the coins of that Emperor. On the lower panels are shown Orientals on one side and Goths on the other. Now, an embassy from India came to Anastasius in 496, and it is doubtless that embassy that is depicted on the ivory; also there was a defeat over the Bulgars in 499 and it may well be these who are shown opposite the Orientals. On these assumptions the ivory has been dated to around 500. Even so, however, some have sought to assign it to Alexandria, though on grounds of historical probability, apart from those of style, this would seem most unlikely.

To the capital again may be attributed the leaf of a diptych now at Liverpool, with three figures above and scenes from the circus below; it has the finish and polish typical of the capital, but in addition to this, Delbrueck has proposed on historical grounds that the three figures at the top almost certainly denote Constantinople.[2] The ivory is to be dated to about 400. The same style appears about fifty years later in a very lovely

[1] Peirce and Tyler, II, pl. 1.
[2] Peirce and Tyler, I, pl. 86. Delbrueck, *Konsulardiptychen*, no. 58.

diptych in the Bargello at Florence, bearing St. Paul at Malta on one leaf and Adam in the garden of Paradise on the other.[1] The animals of the Paradise scene may be compared with some of those on the mosaic floor of the Great Palace. On purely iconographical grounds such a comparison does not furnish very valid evidence as to provenance, for it would seem that mosaic workers and probably ivory carvers too, made very extensive use of manuscripts or sketch-books as models, and some of these must have taken the form of what were virtually animal picture books. They must have been transported over long distances, for only in this way can the very close parallels to be seen between the mosaics of Constantinople and Antioch, Syria and Palestine, Piazza Armerina in Sicily, or numerous places in North Africa, be explained. But even if the iconographic similarity of the animals on the Bargello ivory to those on the Great Palace floor cannot be accepted as sure evidence of provenance, the rather cold style of the carving, the conservatism of the designs and the fine finish of the work may be taken as such an indication, for there is reason to suppose that the "neo-Attic" style, to which this ivory so clearly belongs, is to be associated with Constantinople rather than with any other centre. Delbrueck also supports its Constantinopolitan provenance (no. 69).

Another outstanding ivory which one would tend to associate with the capital on grounds of its quality and excellence is a well-known panel in the British Museum bearing the Archangel Michael (*Byzantine Art*, pl. 49). The "neo-Attic" manner is, however, not quite so much to the fore here; true, the figure is balanced and elegant, but the head is over large, and the eyes have something of that staring character typical of the "expressionist" school; the architectural ornament again is rich and florid, in the manner typical of Syria. The way in which the figure is posed, as if above the earth, with its feet extending over several of the steps on which it stands, savours of the East and is foreign to the Attic tradition. Hinks has described this as the "levitating" treatment,[2] and it serves as an example, not of the incompetence of the artist, as the older school of critics would have us believe, but of the penetration into art of a transcendental conception, which stemmed from the East, but

[1] Peirce and Tyler, I, pl. 124.
[2] *Carolingian Art*, London, 1935, p. 42.

which by the sixth century had become an essential concomitant of Christian art. The figure on the ivory, being angelic, has no need to stand upon such material things as steps; such mundane impedimenta could be set aside, and it is indeed one of the chief glories of these early Christian artists that they set out to disregard things purely material in order to convey the spiritual character of their subject matter, even if the devices to which they had recourse were often somewhat clumsy.

Though few of the other ivories show the influence of the "neo-Attic" style to quite so marked an extent, the manner is to be seen in several of them. One at Brescia, with the name of the Lampadii, depicting a chariot race in a Hippodrome, may serve as an example. The horses thus display the elegance of "neo-Attic" art, but the charioteers are heavy and dumpy, and the three figures watching the races above are coarse and clumsy and assume rigid frontal poses. The ivory has been assigned to Rome by Delbrueck (no. 56) and others. A leaf at Leningrad showing animal combats, probably to be dated to about 450, is in a somewhat similar style, but is perhaps rather to be assigned to Constantinople, for "neo-Attic" traits are more to the fore here than on the Lampadii leaf.

In any discussion of the ivories it is essential to say a word about the most spectacular and best known example of all, the great throne at Ravenna, which bears the monogram of Maximian, who was Archbishop there from 546 to 553 (*Byzantine Art*, pl. 47). It must have been made early in the sixth century. The style of the carvings is not uniform, and at least four hands are to be distinguished. The man who did the panels on the front, which depict the Evangelists and St. John the Baptist, must have been trained in an Asiatic school; the St. John is thus of a Syrian type, and the architectural backgrounds are similar to those of the Lydian sarcophagi, which were carved in Asia Minor. The man who did the scenes from the life of Joseph on the back shows traits of an even more oriental character; the style is dramatic, the costumes are at times distinctly Persian, and the deep niches in which the figures stand are suggestive almost of Graeco-Buddhist art. There are some similarities to Coptic carvings. The New Testament scenes on the back are in a tamer, more pictorial manner, though an oriental, "bird's-eye" type of perspective is employed. The ornamental bands, which show the finest work on the whole chair, again suggest comparison with friezes and scrolls in Syria rather than with those from elsewhere.

These ivories have been assigned to different centres by the various authorities. Antioch has been suggested by some, as has also Constantinople, but Alexandria has found most favour, partly because of the Egyptian character of the third hand, and partly because the iconography is more closely similar to that of the Baouit paintings and other works in Egypt than to anything elsewhere. The prominence given to Joseph in the subject matter has also been cited as an Egyptian feature. Though the case for Alexandria is very strong, the evidence that supports that for Constantinople is not without weight. In the first place it is known that Archbishop Maximian spent some time there; in the second the work of the first hand is fairly closely similar to the decoration of the Barberini ivory; in the third it is more probable that men working in several diverse styles would be found congregated together at the capital rather than anywhere else, for we know that artisans were assembled there by the early Emperors: and finally, even if the carvers worked at Constantinople, it is not necessary to insist that they were all trained there, for all the evidence goes to show that craftsmen moved about very freely at this time. The question certainly cannot be answered here, even if it can be answered at all. All that can be said is that the case for Constantinople is perhaps best supported on general grounds, and that for Alexandria on the basis of iconography and style.[1]

A word must also be said here about the Consular diptychs, an important group of ivories which were issued by consuls on their appointment, much as wedding invitations are issued in the West to-day; indeed, the wedding invitations retain the old form, in that they too have two leaves. They mostly bear the names of the consuls for whom they were made, and they are thus exactly dated. They can also usually be associated either with Rome or Constantinople, for the consuls held office in those places only. It has often been assumed that the ivories were carved in the city in which the consul named on them held

---

[1] Baldwin Smith, "The Alexandrian Origin of the Chair of Maximian", *American Journal of Archaeology*, XXI, 1917, p. 22; C. Cecchelli, *La Cattedra di Massimiano ed altri lavori romano-orientali*, Rome, 1936-44, also favours Alexandria. The case for Constantinople has been best set out by Meyer Schapiro, "The Joseph Scenes on the Maximianus Throne in Ravenna", *Gazette des Beaux Arts*, 40, Paris, 1952, p. 27.

office, but this is not necessarily so, for the style of the carving is not always in close accord with what we believe to be the style characteristic of the place with which it is associated on the basis of the name. One may conclude, therefore, that these things were probably sometimes ordered elsewhere, just as a man appointed to office in London or New York to-day might well buy some particularly important object in Paris. A number of the diptychs are, however, quite definitely to be associated either with Rome or with Constantinople on all grounds. The most important of the former are those of Probus (406), Boethius (487) and Orestes (530), and of the latter those of Areobindus (506), Anastasius (517) and Magnus (518). In each case several examples survive.

In a book which is primarily concerned with painting and mosaic, this has been a long discursus on the subject of sculpture. But where so much of the material has disappeared, especially with regard to the large-scale works, it is essential to take the arts that chance to have been better preserved into account in order to complete the picture. Moreover, there was a very close relationship in iconography and style between works on a large and those on a small scale. Many of the ivories, showing circus scenes, for example, are closely akin to the mosaics of the Great Palace, and there is reason to suppose that small things, and perhaps even ivories, served as models for the larger ones. Thus, in the absence of the large-scale works, the small ones do help very considerably to complete the picture.

With the next chapter, on the other hand, a survey of works on a large scale becomes possible, and the tone of the text will thus change, to become more descriptive and rather less theoretical. But in the author's view the styles and elements that have been discussed in the first three chapters, even though at times only partially represented by surviving examples, were all very essential to the formation of Christian art. And even if not all the works that have been noted were actually Christian, it is, none the less, possible to discern in them features that were to be developed later on in the service of the Christian Church. It was by taking over and selecting from what existed that Christian art was formed, and only when the manner of this selection has been clearly defined can the truly Christian works be adequately examined and discussed. The tale should, logically, be carried on at Constantinople, which was made the capital of the Christian world by Constantine in 330, but that unfortunately is not possible, for practically all the earlier monuments that were set up there have perished, and the early sites still await excavation. In Rome, on the other hand, much survives, and a great deal more has been discovered in recent years, thanks to the painstaking efforts of Italian scholars. It is there, therefore, that our story must be continued, even if at times the art was more conservative and less experimental than that of the new, more progressive, capital on the confines of Europe and Asia.

BOOKS

C. R. Morey, *Early Christian Art*, Princeton, 1942.

H. Peirce and R. Tyler, *Art Byzantin*, Vol. II, Paris.

The Great Palace of the Byzantine Emperors—Reports on excavations by the Walker Trust (St. Andrews), 1947 and 1948.

Part II

THE FIRST FLOWERING

Until quite early in the fourth century Christianity had been no more than a minority faith in the pagan Roman world, and its adherents had indeed often suffered persecution for their beliefs. The whole situation was, however, changed when Constantine adopted the new religion as the official faith of the Roman empire. At the same time he transferred the capital to the shores of the Sea of Marmora, on the very fringe of Europe. The site chosen was that of the old Hellenistic city of Byzantium; it was renamed Constantinople after its founder. Though the architecture, art and daily life of the new city were indebted very considerably to Rome, the inhabitants were mostly of Greek blood, and the position, on the confines of Asia, served to bring it into close touch with the Iranian world. As a result of these factors life, thought and art soon began to develop along distinctive lines, and a new culture came into being, under the influence of the Christian Church. The vicissitudes of time have destroyed much of the art that was produced at Constantinople between the days of Constantine and those of Justinian, the greatest of the eastern emperors, and it is to other places that we must turn for examples of works on a major scale—to Rome, where much was done under the patronage of the Popes, and where a good deal has been preserved; to Ravenna, which was through most of its history in close touch with Constantinople; to Salonica, where much of the artistic production was virtually

Constantinopolitan in character; to other places in the eastern provinces, where work of quality chances to have survived. The works at issue are all Christian in subject matter, though they still belong to what has sometimes been called the "age of formation". With the death of Justinian in 565, however, formation was virtually complete; a new, essentially Christian art had grown to maturity under the patronage of Church and Emperor, and it was during Justinian's reign that some of its most glorious works were produced.

CHAPTER IV

EARLY CHRISTIAN ART IN ROME

WITH the adoption of Christianity as the official religion, art was able, so to speak, to come above ground in the old pagan city of Rome, and painting, instead of being restricted to the decoration of the walls of the Catacombs or of small chambers and chapels, came into use on a large scale in the new churches that were at once set up. At the same time patronage moved from the hands of the poorer classes to the richer, and artists of outstanding quality came to be employed as well as those of obscurer character, who would work for small fees. To wall painting was added the more luxurious art of mosaic; numerous sculptures were done, and minor objects, often in expensive materials, were in addition produced in the service of the Church, so that art production became at the same time both more extensive and more luxurious.

A great deal of the work that was done at this time has of course perished, more especially that in fragile materials, such as textiles or paintings on panels, but a few mosaics of the fourth century and a good many more of the fifth survive in Rome, and there is quite a lot of sculpture, both on a large scale in stone and on a small in ivory. Something has already been said about the ivories, more especially the Consular diptychs, which necessarily form a part of the general picture, though it is not always easy to be sure of where they were made, as they are in a diversity of styles. Here we are concerned not so much with these things as with works which are essentially Christian and also undoubtedly Roman, such as the mosaics and wall painting, which are necessarily immovable, or stone sculptures on a large scale in a material which was carved on the spot and quarried in the neighbourhood.

The earliest of the mosaics are those in the church of Sta Constanza, which was built as an octagonal martyrium or tomb sanctuary between 306 and 337. It was converted into a baptistry in the fifth century, when the lateral apses were added. Only the mosaics on the roofs of the vaulted aisles are of the same date as the original building. This roof is divided into eight compartments, and there are different designs in each, though only those on the three sets on each side survive; they are in pairs, balancing one another on each side (*Byzantine Art*, pl. 3). These mosaics, which consist in the main of scrolls and other diverse motifs shown in isolation against a white ground, are very classical in character; they are virtually floor mosaics transferred to the roof. The mosaics which decorated the central dome have not survived, though there is a sixteenth century painting of them in the Escorial. They included scenes from the Old and New Testaments, bordered below by a river and separated one from another by cariatid figures, not unlike the dividing panels in the Baptistry of the Orthodox at Ravenna. In the apses which terminate the sides of the octagon to the north and south are figural compositions of a rather different character, depicting the "Traditio Legis", where Christ conveys future responsibility for preaching on one side to Peter and on the other to Paul (Pl. 6). Our Lord stands in the centre of each apse, with the Apostle before Him, against a background of trees. The mosaics are probably to be assigned to the time of the building's conversion for use as a baptistry in the fifth century. They have, however, been very much restored at subsequent dates, and to-day appear somewhat clumsy. Those in the dome probably belonged to the same date as those in the vaults of the octagon.

The "landscape" backgrounds of the apse mosaics savour of the "picturesque" style, whereas the scrolls that form the decoration of the Chapel of Sts. Rufinus and Secundus in the Lateran are abstract rather than naturalistic, and include birds, lambs and other pieces of Christian symbolism akin to those in the Catacomb paintings. The work must have been done in the early fifth century, probably under Pope Sixtus III (432-440). The decoration of the apse of Sta Maria Maggiore, before its restoration by Torriti in 1295, must also have consisted of scrolls, though to judge by what survives of them, on either side of Torriti's figures of the Coronation of the Virgin, they were much heavier and more stylised than those in the Lateran Baptistry.

With the decoration of the apse of Sta Pudenziana, done probably between 402 and 417, on the other hand, truly

Rome. Sta Maria Maggiore. Nave mosaic: the Hospitality of Abraham.
432-440. (*Photo Anderson.*)

PLATE 5

Rome.   Sta Constanza.   Mosaic in side niche: the Traditio Legis.   Fifth century.   (*Photo Anderson.*)

PLATE 6

Rome. Sta Pudenziana. Apse mosaic: Christ and the Apostles. 402-417. (*Photo Alinari.*)

PLATE 7

Milan. San Lorenzo. Baptistry. Mosaic in squinch: Christ and Apostles.
355-397. (*Photo Anderson.*)

PLATE 8

Christian work on a grand scale appears for the first time (Pl. 7).[1] Here our Lord is depicted in the centre, with six of the Apostles on either side, one group headed by St. Paul and the other by St. Peter. There are also two female figures, Sta Pudenziana, identified as Ecclesia ex Circumcisione, who is associated with St. Peter, and Sta Praxede, identified with the Ecclesia ex Gentibus, associated with St. Paul. The mosaic has been much restored, but our Lord was probably always a bearded figure, in contrast with the rendering usual in the Catacombs or on the sarcophagi, where He is young and beardless. But the two female figures attest the classical heritage, for they are no more than variants of the personifications so usual in Hellenistic art, while the architectural background is the direct descendant of the architecturescapes that were so popular at Pompeii, and indeed in nearly all secular Roman decorations.

If the ornamental work in all these mosaics attests the influence of the decorations of the pagan period, the sculptures that survive from this age show it equally clearly. There are quite a lot of examples, for it was only at a later date that sculpture fell out of favour as a Christian art, only to be truly revived in Romanesque times. A great many Christian sarcophagi were thus produced in the fourth and fifth centuries, for they replaced the loculi of the Catacombs, in any case among the richer classes, when once the Christian faith was officially recognised. There seem to have been three quite distinct types of Christ in the sculpture of these sarcophagi.[2] The first shows Him in a youthful guise with short curly hair, modelled on an Apollo or similar figure from pagan art. He is shown in this way on the Clipeus sarcophagus in the Lateran Museum (Gerke, pls. 30-35). In the second He is again youthful and beardless, but has long hair, like the young Dionysus; a statue of the seated Christ in the Museo Nazionale (no. 61565; Gerke, pls. 56-59) and one depicting Him as the Good Shepherd, in the Lateran, illustrate this aspect. The latter was perhaps derived from the Hermes Criophorus of classical art. In the third He is long-haired and bearded, like the Philosopher type of antique

---

[1] These mosaics were at one time assigned to the fourth century, but recent research, especially that of Italian scholars, has necessitated a revision of our dating. For a useful summary see A. Calderini, G. Chierici and C. Cecchelli, *La Basilica di S. Lorenzo Maggiore in Milano*, Milan, 1951, p. 250.

[2] For a study of the types of Christ from *c.* 350 onwards, see F. Gerke, *Christus in der Spätantiken Plastik*, Mainz, 1948.

E

art, and is shown no longer as youthful, but as a man of some age. This type of Christ appears both in the Roman world, as for instance on the so-called Jonas sarcophagus in the Lateran (no. 119; Gerke, pl. 7), and in the East, as on the famous Sidamara sarcophagus at Berlin (Fig. 4). Examples of these types are to be found in early paintings also, like those in the Catacombs of Domitilla (Pl. 1), Praetextatus and the Coemeterium of Maius.

Each of these early Christ-types exercised its influence when Christian art began to develop in a distinctive manner, and each of them also left a heritage in later ages. We thus find the youthful, beardless types not only on early sculptures in the south of France and Gaul but also dominating in Carolingian and Ottonian times. The east Christian world, on the other hand, favoured the bearded variant, and as time went on Christ aged perceptibly, so that the conception of Him as a youthful figure was definitely short-lived. Even in Italy, where artists and patrons seem to have wavered undecided between the bearded and the beardless variants down till quite late times, the very youthful Christ disappeared almost with the adoption of Christianity as the official religion. In any case, in the scenes from Christ's life in the nave of S. Apollinare Nuovo or in the apse of San Vitale at Ravenna, Christ is beardless, but is nevertheless a figure of some age and of obvious dignity. By the second half of the fourth century the type of Christ in majesty, beardless in the West and bearded in the East, had come into general favour. In all these works cited so far, however, the classical trend is clearly uppermost, and there are few hints of the "expressionist" rendering which was to be developed so characteristically in Byzantine art, even if at times the liveliness and delicacy of the "picturesque" style gives place to the severer approach of the "neo-Attic".

Next in date among the mosaics is a series of panels in the nave of Sta Maria Maggiore which are to be assigned to the time of Pope Sixtus III; they were possibly brought there from somewhere else. They show Old Testament scenes, in a vivid manner, great attention being paid both to the picturesque aspects of the landscape and the backgrounds, and to the factual record of the story. A scene which was to be reproduced time and again in the story of Christian art, the "Hospitality of Abraham", may serve as an example (Pl. 5). In it the visit of the three angels to Abraham is shown, and the significance of the figures is considerable, in that the three angels frequently came to be regarded as symbols of the Trinity. The panel may be said to represent an admirable blend of the "picturesque" art of the Alexandrine school and the factual narrative art that is to be associated with Rome; it is to be regarded as primarily characteristic of the Italian contribution to early art. The colouring of these scenes is fresh and brilliant, and the compositions lively, and even if there is nothing very profoundly Christian about them, they are none the less very delightful pictures, which will repay a close attention.[1] They serve also to show how very far the development of Old Testament iconography must have gone even before the official adoption of Christianity, and once more attest the importance of the Alexandrine Septuagint illustrations.

The mosaics on the Triumphal Arch in Sta Maria Maggiore are of the same date and are also in the main antique in style, but the subject matter is new, for in place of decorative schemes or subjects connected with the Old Testament the theme is centred upon the Virgin, and it has been suggested that the mosaics were set up in support of the decision taken at the Council of Ephesus of 431, where the teaching of the Nestorians was refuted; they held that the Virgin was to be counted as the Mother of Christ, but not at the same time as the Mother of God. The Popes, all through this controversy as to Christ's nature, which raged with great vigour through these centuries, believed in the duality of His personality, as man and God, and not in the single phase as man only, which was preached by Nestorius.

Whatever inspired Pope Sixtus to commission the work however, there can be no doubt that his mosaicists showed both competence and originality, for many of the scenes must have been new at the time and indeed some of them remain unique in the story of Christian art to this day. One that was to become very important later may however be noted, namely the Hetoimasia or Preparation of the Throne in readiness for the second coming of Christ, following the text of Revelation. The theme achieved early popularity in the West, but was not

---

[1] The mosaics are very high up and need cleaning, and it is perhaps more rewarding to look at the admirable colour plates in Wilpert's book, *Die Römischen Mosaiken und Malereien der kirchlichen Bauten von IV bis XIII Jahrhundert*, 1917, than at the mosaics themselves.

generally adopted in the east Christian world till very much later. The iconography of the mosaics of the Triumphal Arch appears to follow the version of the story known as that of the Pseudo-Matthew, which was popular in the West in the fifth century (*Byzantine Art*, pl. 4). The scenes are shown here in the manner of a continuous narrative, without separations between them, in much the same way that the tale of Trajan's campaigns is told in the reliefs on his column at Rome. This narrative system was very popular in Roman art, but gave place to another manner, usually known as the selective, as Christian art was developed. In this system each scene is shown separately within its own border.

With the exception of some of the figures in the apse of Sta Pudenziana, which have been to a greater or lesser degree refurbished in later times, all these mosaics—and the sculptures of the sarcophagi also—may be said to belong to the classical phase of Christian art. Equally classical in character was the most distinctive type of minor art, that of the famous fonde d'oro glass, where figures in thin gold leaf were inserted between sheets of glass, looking rather like silhouettes. Always an essentially Roman product, the fashion for this glass-ware came to an end with the fifth century. In fact, a seal on this conservative but at times very lovely art was set by the Gothic attacks of the fifth century and the sack of Rome in 410. Such artists of importance as had remained there after the transference of power first to Milan, then to Ravenna seem to have deserted the city for a time at least, and one of the last works that bears an essentially Roman stamp is a manuscript of the works of Dioscorides, now at Vienna, which must be dated to about 512. It bears on its title page a portrait of Julia Anicia, the daughter of Galla Placidia. In addition to this frontispiece, the manuscript contains a portrait of Dioscorides writing his book, as well as a number of pictures of a less monumental character that depict plants and so forth used for medical purposes. The portrait of Dioscorides is not unlike the author portraits of the Evangelists which were later to become so important in Byzantine gospels, while the drawings of plants are the progenitors of a long series of such illustrations in mediaeval times; they were popular in the Islamic world as well as the West.

Such works as were produced in Rome after the first Gothic

attack were mostly either provincial in character or due to the hands of later imigrants who had been trained in Constantinople or Ravenna. Thus the style of the next really outstanding mosaic in Rome, that in the apse of Sts. Cosmas and Damian, is of a very eastern character. It was set up under the patronage of Pope Felix IV (526-530). It shows Christ in the centre, before a background of flame-like clouds, with the Apostle Peter presenting St. Cosmas on one side and the Apostle Paul presenting St. Damian on the other. At the sides stand St. Theodore and Pope Felix, while below is a procession of twelve sheep representing the Apostles, an old piece of symbolism which for long remained very popular in Italy, for we see it followed in most of the later mosaics, as well as in wall paintings like those of Sta Maria in Pallaria (973-977) on the Palatine.

It is, however, the treatment of Christ and the background that constitutes the really important feature of this mosaic. The Christ is a massive, impressive, ageless figure, with long black hair and a thick black beard, who stands poised in space with His arm raised in blessing; the background, with its flame-coloured clouds, seems to extend into limitless space behind. This is not the Christ of humanism; we seem rather to be witnessing a vision, to be assisting at a miracle. Here we see for the first time in art an expression of the esoteric, transcendental faith which was now becoming an essential feature of Christianity, based not so much on the teaching of Christ Himself as on the ideas that had penetrated from the East, together with the arguments and teaching of the Fathers of the Church. In this mosaic a mystic eastern faith is given expression and form in art; here an ideal is exemplified, and we seem to be in the presence of a mystic vision, no longer of this earth, nor limited by its bonds or bounds.

It was along these paths of exploration, in a continued search for the infinite, that Byzantine art was to develop. We see here the full realisation of that trend which was described in our second chapter as the "expressionist", and we see here, exemplified in art, that separation of eastern and western thought which had eventually and inevitably to come about in spite of all attempts that might be made to bridge the gaps between the two areas or to cement the breaches. Here Byzantine art was born. Here we see it in a more developed and distinctive manner than we shall ever see it again on Italian soil, either in the sixth century mosaics of Ravenna or the twelfth century ones of Venice or Sicily.

After the outstanding glory of Sts. Cosmas and Damian, the mosaics set up at subsequent dates in quite a number of churches at Rome come as rather a disappointment, especially when compared to work done elsewhere. Yet there is a more or less continuous series of them, over three centuries, which is something unparalleled in any other region. The most important are those in San Lorenzo (578-580), Sta Agnese (625-638), Sta Maria in Cosmedin (705-707), Sta Maria in Domnica, Sta Cecilia, Sta Praxede (all 817-824), San Marco (827-844) and Sta Maria in Trastevere (1139-1153). All of these mosaics are rather wooden and clumsy; the degree of "Byzantinism" varies, but the eastern type of Christ, with black hair and beard, is universal, and the costumes and similar accoutrements of the figure are in most cases of Byzantine type. A good many of the mosaics would appear to have been set up at the time of Iconoclasm (726-843), when the depiction of the saintly or divine form in art was forbidden in the eastern world by imperial decree, though the ban never extended to the West. It has been suggested that some of these mosaics were set up as a sort of tangible witness to representation in sacred art, and some of them may even have been the work of Greek craftsmen who came to the West as refugees. But if this was so, they can hardly have been the best craftsmen available, for the work as a whole savours of provincialism. In San Lorenzo, for example, the Christ seems almost a puppet in contrast to the figure in Sts. Cosmas and Damian, and the Saints and Bishops on either side seem as if frozen. The mosaic in the apse of Sta Agnese, with the patron saint of the church between the Popes Symmachus and Honorius, is more satisfactory, but is, nevertheless, rather weak. The apse of Sta Praxede, with Christ, Saints and Pope Pascal I, is fussy, while the figures in the apse of Sta Maria in Domnica, Sta Cecilia and San Marco are crowded and stereotyped. A few compositions on a smaller scale are of higher quality. Individual figures like the Saints in San Pietro in Vinculi (c. 680) may be noted, and a fragmentary adoration in Sta Maria in Cosmedin (705-707) is fine, but even these pale before the earlier works in Rome or later ones in the East.

Perhaps the best of all are the mosaics that decorate the chapel of San Zeno in the church of Sta Praxede (817-824), where a glorious deep blue dominates the colouring and where a profoundly spiritual feeling seems to embrace the observer when he enters. The chapel is quite small, and its walls and vaulted roof are entirely covered with mosaics. At the centre of the roof is a bust of the Saviour, upheld by four tall angels, placed diagonally. On the walls are subjects of a rather symbolical character: the four rivers of paradise, the divine lamb, the throne adored by Sts. Peter and Paul, and so on. The chapel is dark and the cubes of the mosaic are set rather unevenly so that they produce a curious scintillating effect, lovely and moving in itself but ineffective in a photographic reproduction.

But if these later mosaics in Rome are on the whole disappointing, some of the wall paintings in the city are a good deal more subtle, and comprise among them works of real quality. They indicate very clearly that there was a revival of artistic energy in the eighth century, corresponding to an expansion of Roman teaching in the West and the decline of the old Celtic Church, and this revival was of course accentuated by the coronation of Charlemagne as Emperor of the West in the year 800. These paintings will be considered in a subsequent chapter. Here the rather earlier ones in Sta Maria Antiqua in the Forum may be noted (see p. 111 f.). Work here is in various styles, varying from the Italian to the Byzantine and the Eastern. A very eastern rendering of the Crucifixion, where Christ wears a long robe or colobium is interesting; it is normally associated with this scene only in Syria and Palestine; in the Constantinopolitan sphere Christ invariably wears the Greek loincloth. This painting may be compared with the rendering on the small reliquary, probably painted in Palestine, which has already been mentioned (p. 35), or with an illustration in the Rabula Gospels at Florence, which were written and illustrated at Zagba in Mesopotamia in 586. Either an eastern model was used, or some eastern artist must have found his way to Rome. Perhaps the Alexandrines who worked in the picturesque style were not the only painters who were driven westwards by the Moslem invaders?

The ninth century, which happens to be the date at which Sta Maria Antiqua was destroyed, also saw a turning-point in the history of art in the city and the rest of Italy, for practically all the works of later date are in a different style, and belong to western mediaeval art rather than to the phase we describe as Early Christian. Many of them are, nevertheless, quite important, and all are interesting.

BOOKS

E. W. ANTHONY, *Romanesque Frescoes*, Princeton, 1951.

W. WEIDLE, *Mosaïques paléochrétiennes et byzantines*, Milan-Florence, 1954.

M. VAN BERCHEM and E. CLUZOT, *Mosaïques chrétiennes*, Geneva, 1924.

CHAPTER V

EARLY CHRISTIAN ART IN THE REST OF ITALY

ROME, as we have seen, remained one of the principal centres in the production of mosaics and sculpture for a century or more after the transference of the capital to Constantinople in 330, but this importance waned as the fifth century progressed, owing firstly to the growing importance of the new capital, and secondly to the situation in Italy itself, which saw the attacks of Goths from the north, who were able to penetrate to and eventually to sack Rome in 410. True, the sack had no very marked or lasting effect on art, for it did not greatly accelerate a movement towards provincialism which had already set in. In the rest of Italy, however, or rather in the other important centres in the rest of Italy, the provincialism was rather less marked, and at Ravenna especially, and in a few other places also, work of a really outstanding character was produced from the early fifth century down to the middle of the sixth. And even before that, fine things were being done in other places, notably Milan.

The mosaics that decorate the chapel of St. Aquilino, adjoining the church of San Lorenzo there, are of particular interest. They resemble to some extent those of Sta Maria Maggiore in Rome, but are probably to be assigned to a rather earlier date; one between 355 and 397 has recently been suggested. They are, unfortunately, very fragmentary, but enough survives to show their quality and very great interest. The walls of the vestibule of the Baptistry must originally have been adorned with figures of saints and apostles, standing within an elaborate architectural framing of rather Pompeiian character. To-day only a few vestiges of this decoration survive, but enough is there to show the brilliance of the colours, and in addition certain stylistic features are to be noted, such as the inclusion of a small triangular shadow rather like a leaf behind each of the feet; similar leaf-like shadows appear on many of the early floor mosaics, and their occurrence here is one of the factors that attests the early date of the San Lorenzo ones. The use of such naturalistic features was something quite foreign to the Byzantine outlook.

In the baptistry itself—as opposed to the vestibule—mosaics originally decorated the four conch-shaped squinches; the mosaics of the south-east conch are preserved entirely and those of the north-east one in part. In the one is Christ in the midst of the Apostles (Pl. 8); the figures are well disposed and the composition extremely dignified. In the other is a scene which Wilpert interprets as a chariot of glory, drawn by horses; if its connotation is Christian, its iconography is drawn directly from a classical source, that of the sun-chariot of Helios. In the corners are shepherds with their flocks. The work here is especially effective and full of delightful details. A sleeping shepherd fits ideally into the right-hand corner.

In addition to its very great artistic qualities, this mosaic is also especially interesting on account of the evidence it furnishes regarding the method of work. In places where the tesserae have fallen the setting bed has been laid bare and the outline drawing which was used by the mosaicist is visible. The scene does not seem to have been coloured in paint here, as was usually the case in the Constantinopolitan mosaics at a later date, only the general outline was indicated, in black paint. Perhaps the more impressionistic technique employed here, where each individual cube contrasted with its neighbour, called for a different treatment to that required when the different colours of the mosaic were laid in larger areas or in continuous, ordered lines, as was the practice in later Byzantine work.

Milan was also important as a centre of ivory carving. The ivories that are to be assigned there indeed constitute a definite group, of which a panel at Munich, bearing the Ascension, and a plaque with the three Marys at the tomb, in the Trivulzio collection in Milan itself, are the most typical pieces.[1] The former is perhaps as early as the beginning of the fifth century. The style is "neo-Attic", but purely factual elements are stressed to a greater degree than was usual in the East, and more

---

[1] See Volbach, Salles, Duthuit, *Art Byzantin*, pl. 15, c, or Peirce and Tyler, I, pl. 96, for the Munich plaque, and Molinier, pl. VI, or Morey, *Early Christian Art*, p. 145, for the one in the Trivulzio collection.

attention is paid to the narrative aspect. Christ is thus drawn up into heaven by the hand of the Father in a most practical and material manner, which is quite distinct from the imaginative conception that dominated in the Byzantine world. The iconography is also different from that which was developing in the East, for three women are shown, in accordance with Mark's version, whereas in the East there were usually two, in accordance with Matthew's. In fact, both iconography and style are distinct, and the heritage of those highly realistic bas-reliefs which were so popular in later pagan art in Rome is clearly demonstrated in the ivories.

Four plaques in the British Museum, showing the Bearing of the Cross, the Crucifixion, the Marys at the Sepulchre and the Incredulity of Thomas, have also sometimes been assigned to Milan; in this case the work is coarser than on the Munich and Trivulzio plaques, and Gaul seems a more likely home.[1] Two other works on a rather larger scale which show stylistic relationship with the Milan ivories may also be mentioned. Both bear a closely similar series of Old and New Testament scenes. There is no reason why one, an ivory casket now at Brescia, should not have been carved at Milan, for it is very similar to the plaques. The other has sometimes been assigned to Milan, but Rome seems a more likely home, for the finished work is on a large scale, consisting of the wooden panels that compose the doors of Sta Sabina. The doors were set up in 432, when the church was dedicated. There seems no reason why such things should have been brought from far away at a time when there were certainly artists available in Rome itself quite capable of carving them. Moreover, these sculptures show close resemblances to the reliefs of the arcaded sarcophagi, which were done at Rome without doubt. The choice of scenes on the doors is interesting, for those from the Old Testament were selected as parallels to those from the New; for example the Marriage at Cana and the Loaves and Fishes are paralleled by Moses' miracles of the quails, and the manna and of drawing water from the Rock. This system of juxtaposition was by no means unusual in Christian art at a subsequent date.

Another school of artists seems to have existed at the same time in the south of Italy. No ivories have so far been attributed

---

[1] Morey, *Mediaeval Art*, p. 75. See also Baldwin Smith, *Early Christian Iconography and the School of Provence*, 1918.

to this region, but several extensive mosaic decorations were set up in the fifth century, of which the most important that survives is in the Baptistry of Soter at Naples, which is perhaps to be dated as early as the end of the fourth century. There is a more fragmentary decoration at Capua which is closely similar to the Naples mosaic in style though it is certainly rather later in date. In the former, ornamental bands radiated from a central medallion, dividing the roof into eight compartments which were filled with scenes from the New Testament; below in niches were the symbols of the four Evangelists. The work is rather coarse and the palette more limited than at Milan.

By the middle of the fifth century, however, the main centre of initiative had really become concentrated at Ravenna, and a whole series of very outstanding mosaics were set up there from about 420 onwards, most of which are still well preserved. Even if the purist may object that many of them have been overmuch restored, it is probably easier to gather at Ravenna a convincing idea of what the artists of this age were capable than at any other place.

It was as a result of the division of control between joint emperors ruling in East and West that Ravenna achieved its importance, and it was thanks to the close contacts between the two courts that work at Ravenna attained such high quality. It is this factor, more than any other, which makes Ravenna more interesting and more important than any other place in Italy. Even when the city was under Gothic rule the same high standards of work were maintained, and indeed some of the most important mosaics there are those in the basilica of S. Apollinare Nuovo, done under the patronage of Theodoric.

The mosaics that survive at Ravenna can be conveniently grouped into three periods, the first that of Galla Placidia (c. 420-450), the second that of Theodoric (493-526), and the third that of Justinian (527-565). During the first of these the city was the capital of the west Roman empire, though it was in close touch with Constantinople owing to the duality of rule; during the second it was an independent principality under the control of a Gothic ruler, who sought to assimilate the culture of Byzantium; during the third it was no more than a provincial outpost of the great Byzantine empire, with government, wealth and patronage centred at the capital (Constantinople) to a degree hardly experienced before, even in the most prosperous days of Roman imperialism; yet even then work of high quality was done. The art of each of these phases reflects the prevailing conditions to a surprisingly marked degree.

Of the first period the most complete monument is the Mausoleum of Galla Placidia (about 440); no more glorious unity than this small cruciform chapel could be conceived. It contains two major figural compositions, the martyrdom of St. Lawrence in the lunette at the east and Christ the Good Shepherd in that at the west, over the entrance (Pl. 10). Beside the windows are the Apostles, two on each side; at the ends of the transepts are lovely compositions of deer drinking, among formal scrolls; on the vaults of the transepts are vine scrolls rising from acanthus leaves, and on the nave vaults are rosettes and stars in gold on a deep blue ground; in the dome is a cross among stars, with the symbols of the four Evangelists in the corners. The Good Shepherd panel is perhaps the most successful of all these as a composition, for it is a very lovely picture, as well as a work of profound faith. The heritage of the "picturesque" tradition is clearly apparent in the whole conception as well as in such details of the subject matter as the rocks, the sheep, the trees and the plants; our Lord, youthful, beardless and long-haired, attests the survival of a classical idiom, though He is already quite obviously the Christian Saviour. As a composition the St. Lawrence is less perfect, though it is interesting as an illustration of the development of a new iconographical theme—the Saint with his gridiron—at so early a date after the adoption of Christianity. The decorative work on the other hand, though less interesting to the western mind than that possessed of subject matter, is nevertheless outstandingly fine and the colours are of a depth and loveliness seldom realised in subsequent work; the deer and the scrolls that surround them may be noted in particular. The whole interior constitutes, with its gold and deep blue, a symphony in sheer colour which thereafter remained unequalled in the story of art.

The mosaics of the Baptistry of the Orthodox, which are to be assigned to between 425 and 458, are richer in that the colour is more varied and the subject matter more elaborate; but they do not achieve quite the same symphonic effect. Above, at the centre of the dome, is the Baptism, with gold background, and, in the next register, the twelve Apostles, against deep blue backgrounds. Below are a series of architectural compositions, separated by candelabra-like columns in gold, each of them framing an allegorical scene signifying the preparation of the throne (Pl. A). These mosaics are rather earlier than those in the dome. Below, there is an arch in each section of the octagon with a window at its centre. Above each window are deer and scrolls painted in grisaille, and at either side a full-length figure in a plaster niche. Each side of the lowest storey again consists of an arch, supported on free-standing columns; within, marble revetment panels and mosaics alternate one with the other; above the arches are further scrolls in mosaic, with the Apostles in each corner above the columns. There is only one scene here that forms a picture like the Good Shepherd in the Mausoleum of Galla Placidia, but the general effect is one of amazing richness, and the details are particularly satisfying in the sheer delight and brilliance of their colour. This is especially the case with the compositions representing the Hetoimasia or Preparation of the Throne for the second coming. Whereas at Galla Placidia gold and deep blue are the predominating shades, here greens, yellows, red, and indeed every colour conceivable in glass mosaic also have a part to play. The scene of the Baptism at the centre of the dome is most effectively rendered, and the figures of the Apostles are full of life and movement, but it is really the architectural compositions on the middle registers that constitute the most lovely part of the decoration; they serve to show how very impressive and beautiful art without figures could be.

Only the mosaics of the actual dome survive in the other of the Ravennate baptisteries, that of the Arians, better known as Sta Maria in Cosmedin. The figures of the Apostles are more rigid and the attitudes of Christ and St. John in the Baptism scene are somewhat awkward and unconvincing, though the general effect is colourful and decorative. They were done around the year 500 and so belong to the next phase of Ravennate art. The work is in some ways more barbaric and serves as an indication of how quickly quality could decline if the demands of patronage failed to set the highest standards.

The most important mosaics of the age of Theodoric, however, are the scenes from the life and Passion of Christ above the windows on the nave walls of S. Apollinare Nuovo, set up about 504 (Pl. 9, a). Each scene is shown as a separate picture,

A. Ravenna. Baptistry of the Orthodox. Detail. 425-430. (*Photo Powell.*)

which tells its story effectively and straightforwardly in the prosaic style proper to Roman art; there is little of that transcendentalism or search for profound expression which characterises the eastern Mediterranean. Without being wooden like the Apostles in the Arian Baptistry, the figures are rather solid and dumpy; but they tell the story vividly and with astonishing effect. Christ is beardless in the scenes from His life, but bearded in those from the Passion; the variation indicates the birth of a new outlook, which conceived of Him as a figure of dignity rather than of intimacy. As yet the conception only extends to His latter days, when the ceremony of trial and ordeal of death were at hand. But soon this conception was to govern ideas of His nature as a man, so that even in the early scenes from His life He was shown bearded. Eventually a similar comprehension came to govern His depiction even as a child, for though the scale was reduced, the face was dignified and mature, and in no way childlike.

The single figures between the windows in S. Apollinare belong to the same date, but the processions of saints below represent the last important phase of work at Ravenna, that of Justinian. On one side the procession is of female saints, headed by the Magi, and leads from the city of Classis to the Virgin; on the other it is of males, who move from Ravenna to Christ. Between the figures are palm trees, which add to the decorative effect even if they detract somewhat from the movement. The three Magi are especially effective (Pl. 9, *b*). The work is freer than that of Theodoric's day, and the figures are more delicate. The taste of a new age of brilliance, luxury and culture is already apparent, even though the processions can only have been done a few years later than the Bible scenes above them.

Two other outstanding decorations characterise the new age even more completely, namely those of San Vitale and S. Apollinare in Classe. The mosaics in the former church comprise Old Testament scenes, portrayals of the Evangelists (Pl. 12), and the famous panels of Justinian and Theodora and their courts, all of which are in the projecting presbytery at the east end. In the apse is a lovely composition showing Christ enthroned on the orb of the world, between two angels, with Archbishop Ecclesius on one side and the patron saint, St. Vitale, on the other. Christ, short-haired and beardless, is clearly modelled on a classical figure, and the ground, richly decorated with flowers and plants, savours of the "picturesque" style, but the angels and bishops are massive and expressive, and there is an entirely new formalism of an abstract character in the details and the backgrounds of the Old Testament scenes. Buildings which derive from the old architecturescapes are, it is true, present, especially in the scene of Abel and Melchizedek, but they are less important than the clouds in the sky, which have something of the abstract quality of those in Sts. Cosmas and Damian at Rome, while the corresponding scene on the opposite side of the presbytery is so crammed with incident (Abraham; Sarah and the three angels; the sacrifice of Abraham), that there is no room for background.

In the two famous panels of Justinian and Theodora on the apse walls change towards an art of a new type has gone very much further (*Byzantine Art*, pl. 10). The figures are posed frontally, the costumes fall in severe parallel folds, and there is an interest in colour, pattern and ornament for its own sake which is unknown in any of the works produced elsewhere in Italy up to this time. Breasted chose for the book in which he described the discovery of the Dura paintings of A.D. 85 the title, *Oriental Forerunners of Byzantine Painting*, and one can see here clearly enough both the reason for his choice of title and the results of the oriental influence. Indeed, except for a few details of costume and portraiture, the style of the classical world has here given way to something else, which is quite definitely a new style, and one of great importance, though its ends and aims are distinct. In some ways one might describe these mosaics as the first truly Byzantine works at Ravenna, just as the apse of Sts. Cosmas and Damian is the first at Rome.

The construction of San Vitale was begun by Archbishop Ecclesius (524-534)—hence his portrait in the apse. It was completed by Maximian, Justinian's Archbishop, about 547, and most of the decoration was done under his patronage also. Maximian probably made a journey to Constantinople before his appointment as Bishop, and it is possible that he brought back workmen with him; if so, that would account for the rather more conservative character of the apse, perhaps the first work to be put in hand, and the more advanced nature of the portrait panels. Perhaps he also brought back at the same time some of the ivories which compose the famous throne that bears his name. Many of the panels in any case have assembly marks in

Ravenna. S. Apollinare Nuovo. Mosaics in Nave: (*a*) Christ before Pilate.
520-530. (*b*) The Magi present their gifts. *c*. 540. (*Photos Alinari*.)

PLATE 9

Ravenna. Mausoleum of Galla Placidia. Christ the Good Shepherd. *c. 440.* (*Photo Alinari.*)

PLATE 10

Reliquary from the Sancta Sanctorum.   Five scenes from the New Testament.
Sixth century.   (*Photo Vatican Library.*)

PLATE 11

Ravenna. San Vitale. The Evangelist Matthew, 526-547. (*Photo Alinari.*)

PLATE 12

Parenzo Cathedral.   Apse mosaic: the Virgin.   Early sixth century.
(*Photo Alinari.*)

PLATE 13

(a) The Vienna Genesis. Jacob and his flocks. *c*. 500. (*After Gerstinger.*)

(b) The Rossano Codex. The Raising of Lazarus. Mid sixth century.
(*After Munoz.*)

PLATE 14

Greek characters, so they were certainly not carved in Italy. As a whole the throne is a most imposing work,[1] and many of the plaques that go to compose it are of outstanding quality as ivory carvings (see p. 56).

Before discussing the last great mosaic at Ravenna, that of S. Apollinare in Classe, another mosaic of slightly earlier date should perhaps be mentioned, namely that in the apse of the basilica at Parenzo, on the opposite shore of the Adriatic. It must have been set up by workmen from Ravenna somewhere around 540. The Virgin is shown enthroned at the centre of the conch of the apse, for the first time in Christian art. There is an angel on her either side, and beyond the angel are saints, who include Bishop Euphrasius, the founder, and behind him Claudius, his Archdeacon (Pl. 13). Below, on the vertical wall of the apse, are the Annunciation and the Visitation; and between the windows are angels and saints; above, outside the apse, Christ sits enthroned on a globe, with six Apostles on either side. This panel is perhaps later than the rest, for the figures are rather wooden, and savour somewhat of later work at Rome, whereas those on the walls of the apse itself show movement and expression and are finely done. The main composition in the conch is grand and dignified, though the quality is by no means as high as in San Vitale.

The last work on a really extensive scale at Ravenna is the apse mosaic of S. Apollinare in Classe; it dates from about 549 (*Byzantine Art*, pl. 6). On the triumphal arch above is a bust of Christ in a medallion, against a background of clouds. He is supported by the four figures of Ezechiel's vision, the lion, the bull, the man and the eagle, which subsequently became identified respectively with the Evangelists St. Mark, St. Luke, St. Matthew and St. John. Below are the Apostles, symbolised by lambs, which issue from buildings representing Bethlehem and Jerusalem. Below again, on either side, there is a tall palm tree—a gorgeous piece of decoration, admirably suited to the space it has to fill—and below again there is, on either side, an archangel, standing full-face, in a costume made out of a richly decorated silk; similar archangels appear in numerous works of later date, for example in the mosaics at Nicaea and in Sancta Sophia at Constantinople, but they wear either imperial robes or costumes of a more classical character. The costumes of the

---

[1] L. Bréhier, *Sculpture et arts mineurs*, pls. xxvii and xxviii.

F

S. Apollinare archangels indicate once more the degree of penetration of eastern ideas at this time, which is more obviously apparent in the Justinian and Theodora panels in San Vitale.

On the vertical walls of the apse four archbishops of Ravenna appear between the windows, the canopied niches in which they stand being depicted in mosaic with great realism. Beyond them are portrait groups of Justinian and Theodora, similar to but less successful than those in San Vitale. But the real glory of the composition is in the conch above, where the Transfiguration is represented by means of symbolism. At the centre is a great jewelled cross—the transfigured Christ—with a prophet in clouds on either side. The three Apostles who accompanied our Lord are represented as sheep, two on one side and one on the other. They stand amongst the trees and flowers of a gay and colourful landscape. Below again, the twelve are shown as in Sts. Cosmas and Damian at Rome, in the guise of sheep, while S. Apollinare stands with his arms raised in prayer at the centre.

From the point of view of the technique, the brilliance of the colouring, and the richness of the presentation, this mosaic is obviously to be connected with a great and prosperous patron like Justinian. But the subject matter shows a curious blend of ideas. The landscape, the praying figure, the sheep, and the aniconic rendering of the scene of the Transfiguration all seem to hark back to the art of the Catacombs. In its symbolism the mosaic shows far less influence of the trend of ideas which had come to characterise Byzantine religious art and religious thought by this time than do other compositions at Ravenna. In this respect the apse of Sts. Cosmas and Damian at Rome has progressed to a greater degree. The S. Apollinare in Classe mosaic shows most clearly that development was not uniform, and that artists who worked at the same dates and even in the same places were at times more conservative, at times more progressive. But if any lesson, in addition to this, is to be learnt at Ravenna, it is with regard to the role of patronage, for, whatever the subject matter, the styles of Justinian's, Theodoric's and Galla Placidia's foundations are all quite distinct one from the other. Even a superficial acquaintance with them shows this clearly. There were great changes between about 440 and about 540, and these monuments serve to prove that Christian art was not dead and static, but rather was possessed of a great vigour and energy which occasioned its development at every age and period.

The few other mosaics at Ravenna, one in the Archbishop's Palace and one from the Church of S. Michele in Affricisco, which is now at Berlin, need not detain us, for, though interesting, they add little to the general story. Such other mosaics as there are outside Ravenna are all of a later date, and are also outside the scope of this chapter; the same is true of the paintings that survive. They will be dealt with in due course, either as offshoots of the Byzantine school associated with Constantinople, or as early manifestations of the schools that were to develop under Carolingian or subsequent patronage in the West.

BOOKS

E. W. ANTHONY, *A History of Mosaics*, Boston, 1935.

G. BOVINI, *Mosaici di Ravenna*, Milan, 1956; an English edition is in preparation.

O. G. VON SIMSON, *Sacred Fortress*, Chicago, 1948.

CHAPTER VI

CONSTANTINOPLE AND THE EASTERN MEDITERRANEAN

HAD all the works that were set up at Constantinople between about 500 and 700 been preserved, a very long chapter would have been required to deal with them even in a most summary manner. But owing to Iconoclasm in the seventh and eighth centuries, when works of art representing saintly or divine figures in human form were torn down, to the sack of the city after the Latin conquest of 1204, to the Turkish conquest of 1453, and above all, to the fact that Constantinople has always been a flourishing city with a rich population which constantly wished to build anew rather than to restore, very little indeed remains from early times. The mosaic floor of the Great Palace which was described in the third chapter had been covered over and the building to which it belonged reconstructed within little more than a hundred years of its setting; the original decoration of Sancta Sophia was almost entirely removed by the Iconoclasts two centuries after the building's erection, and the same must have been true of those in the other churches. The Great Palace itself was continually reconstructed and enlarged, and when Constantine Porphyrogenitus wrote his famous description of it in the early tenth century it had taken on an entirely different appearance from that which characterised it in the sixth, at the time of Justinian. The houses of the nobles were no doubt similarly rebuilt, for the eight centuries that comprise the period between Justinian and the fall of Byzantium to Islam represent a long space of time in the history of any style, and even if Byzantine art was conservative in comparison, say, to the art of Renaissance Italy, Byzantine culture was far from static; nor was Byzantine history one of a long progressive decline as Gibbon conceived it. Our own society has no doubt developed more rapidly, but there is not very much in the spheres of decorative or minor

arts that has been continually in service that is now more than
four centuries old, let alone eight hundred years!

In view of all this, the story of painting and mosaic at
Constantinople is an obscure one, and practically the only thing
of the period that is known is a fragmentary mosaic made up
of great acanthus scrolls in an upper chamber of Sancta Sophia.
It has recently been uncovered by the expedition working there
on behalf of the Byzantine Institute of America. The evidence
suggests that this mosaic was set up when certain alterations
were made to the building by Justin II (565-578). In order to
gather a picture of what was done in the way of mosaic and
painting during these centuries it is necessary on the one hand
to go farther afield and examine what survives elsewhere, more
especially at Salonica, a city which was always in close relationship with the capital, and on the other to take the other arts
into account, more especially the sculpture. Happily quite a
lot of material on a large scale is preserved in the Museum of
Antiquities at Istanbul, and it is of a nature that enables us to
make deductions as to the character of church art at the time;
it presents a very different picture from that which would be
afforded by a study of such things as the Consular diptychs
alone. A good deal of this sculpture is, moreover, of real quality,
and it comprises a wide series of styles and decorates very
diverse objects, such as sarcophagi, closure slabs, capitals,
pilasters and pulpits. There are even a few free-standing
figures, though these were generally speaking rare in the
Byzantine world.

Some of these sculptures, like the great imperial sarcophagi
made for Constantine and his immediate successors, are in
imported materials, like porphyry or green marble (verde
antica). But most numerous and most characteristic of
Constantinopolitan work as a whole are sculptures in local
materials, notably a rather coarse limestone quarried on the
mainland near by and a fine white marble brought by sea from
the Marmora Islands only a few hours' journey away. Work in
the former is naturally coarser than that in the latter, but often
has a sincerity and a sort of rugged freshness which redeems the
clumsiness; some slabs from the church of St. John of Studion
at Constantinople showing Old Testament scenes are in their
way fine and impressive (Fig. 8). They are to be dated to the
fifth century. Work in marble of the same date is more finished

Fig. 8. Sculptured slab from the church of St. John Studion, Constantinople.

and polished, but like much that was done in the "neo-Attic" style tends to be rather cold and severe. But sculpture in limestone and marble alike shows similar changes in outlook from age to age. Flat, low relief and a linear treatment gradually supplanted a three-dimensional, truly sculptural approach, till eventually capitals were exclusively decorated with an all-over ornament, achieving its effect in the same way as a silhouette. Large flat slabs with floral, animal or geometric motifs of a stylised formal character also became popular. By the seventh century these were the only types of sculpture produced in the Byzantine world, high relief or free-standing work having totally disappeared. The slabs were used in the lower registers of windows, or in the screens between choir and presbytery which from the sixth century onwards played an essential role in church architecture. The introduction of "The Great Entry" into the ecclesiastical ritual in the time of Justin II (565-578) had led to the introduction of these screens, and they became more extensive and more solid as time went on, till they were eventually transformed into the high-wooden iconostases which are now universal in the Orthodox world.[1]

Of the fifth or sixth century sculptures of a more ambitious type, a number of outstanding pieces are preserved in the Museum of Antiquities at Istanbul. One of the most important is a great ambon or pulpit from Salonica which must be dated to the fifth century. There are eight niches on its curved face, separated by Corinthian columns, and within these stand the Virgin, the kings of the East, and the shepherds; together these illustrate the scene of the Adoration. It is an important piece, for not only is the form something new, and essentially Christian—unlike the sarcophagi—but also the whole spirit of the carving attests the birth of new ideas. The way in which the leaves are treated is thus distinctive, and the ornamental frieze above the figures heralds the "light-and-dark" geometric ornament typical of Justinianic sculpture, for example in the capitals of Sancta Sophia at Constantinople or San Vitale at Ravenna (Fig. 9). The treatment of the ornamental work on the Salonica ambon and the more advanced stage of this manner that we see on the Justinianic capitals has often been termed "colouristic", in that it is the black-and-white pattern

---

[1] For a study of the earlier type of screen, see J. W. Crowfoot, *Early Churches in Palestine*, London, 1941.

that produces the effect, rather than relief properly speaking. The ultimate result of the development of this technique was the production of pierced work, and pierced slabs actually became very popular from the sixth century onwards. But

FIG. 9.   Capital, Sancta Sophia, Constantinople.   532-537.

this line of development, though technically perhaps the most original, was not that which led to the most important results from the artistic, one might almost say also from the Christian, point of view, for the patterns most suitable to pierced work were necessarily limited to those of a geometric character, and figural work was an impossibility. It was instead in the development of work in low relief of a rather linear character that the most interesting Byzantine contribution to sculpture was made. The fine-grained white marble of the Marmora Islands lent itself particularly well to this technique.

The earliest examples to show the Byzantine low relief style in a fully developed state are probably a pair of slabs from the sides of an ambon staircase from Aidin, now in the Museum of Antiquities at Istanbul[1] (Fig. 10). They are to be assigned to

---

[1] Mendel, *Catalogue des sculptures*, nos. 645 and 646.

Fig. 10. Side of ambon from Aidin. Sixth century.
Museum of Antiquities, Istanbul.

the early sixth century. On one, Christ is shown as the Good Shepherd with a dog behind Him and a lamb on His shoulders; on the other a figure—perhaps also the Good Shepherd—stands beside a tree. Both, but especially the latter, may be compared with the silver plates made at Constantinople and now in the Hermitage (see p. 51); and though the sculptures came from Aidin, they may be counted as typically Constantinopolitan work of the "neo-Attic" style. From such a piece as this to the numerous slabs with stylised figural work in low relief done between the sixth and the ninth centuries the step was a direct one.

The slabs bear animals, birds or figures of a more direct Christian iconography, such as individual saints or, more especially, the Virgin. There are several fine ones in the Istanbul museum which illustrate the line of development, and there are numerous kindred examples elsewhere. The only real difficulty is to date them exactly. For example, it may be questioned whether the slab from Adalia bearing the archangel Michael, which Peirce and Tyler illustrate and assign to the sixth century, is really so early[1]; it might equally well belong to the tenth century. Nor is it very much easier to date what is perhaps the most important piece of Byzantine sculpture that has come down to us, namely the ciborium arch from the church of St. Mary Panachrantos, which bears in high relief the busts of the twelve Apostles (Fig. 11). Some of the heads are still distinctly Roman in style, but the ornamental details and the costumes are already completely Byzantine. The sixth and the early tenth century have both been proposed, and both dates are possible on stylistic and archaeological grounds. The earlier date seems on the whole the more likely. The church in its present form was consecrated in 908, but the remains of an earlier building have been found below it. The style of these sculptures, however, contrasts with that of certain busts of the Apostles of the fifth century in the Istanbul museum which Pierce and Tyler have termed the elephantine.[2]

There is every reason to believe that all these sculptures, whether early or late, were carved either in Constantinople or in the neighbouring islands of the Marmora, where the quarries were—and that comes to much the same thing. They provide

[1] Peirce and Tyler, II, pl. 32.
[2] *Op. cit.*, I, pl. 87.

an accurate, albeit incomplete, picture of the sacred art of the capital, which was clearly less conservative than the secular art, as illustrated by the silver vessels mentioned in a previous chapter. The two or three manuscripts that survive from this period help to complete our picture, and show how art and iconography were developing during this age, but here it is less easy

FIG. 11.   Figures from the ciborium arch, church of St. Mary Panachrantos, Constantinople.   Sixth century.   Museum of Antiquities, Istanbul.

to be sure of what was actually done in the city, for even if many authorities accept the attribution of these manuscripts to Constantinople, others have disputed their provenance. Thus the Vienna Genesis has been assigned to Alexandria, Asia Minor, Syria, Rome and "the West", as well as to Constantinople, while the Rossano Codex has been attributed to southern Italy, Asia Minor, Antioch and Constantinople; a third manuscript, the "Sinope fragment", in the Bibliothèque

Nationale, has been more generally accepted as Syrian, and a fourth, the Cotton Genesis in the British Museum, was probably done in Alexandria. In the Vienna Genesis oriental traits are marked in spite of the great monumentality of many of the illuminations; they are less to the fore in the Rossano Codex. Such manuscripts as these undoubtedly exercised a great influence on the development of Christian art and Christian iconography, for the manuscripts were easily transportable and were no doubt used as models for works on a larger scale.

The Vienna Genesis shows the work of several hands; Morey actually distinguishes six.[1] One at least was very clumsy. One worked in an essentially "picturesque" manner, favouring perspective backgrounds, but had real command of life and movement; his animals, like those in the scene of Jacob and his flocks, suggest that he was a keen observer of nature, though he made use of earlier models for the basis of his compositions (Pl. 14, a). A third artist liked a more formal and severe arrangement, but his work is not without distinction; Isaac and Abimelech may be assigned to him. There are hints of all our three styles in this manuscript: "picturesque" details, "expressionist" figures and grand compositions, and the painters must have been trained in different schools. But all must have made considerable use of the Septuagint roll. Stylistically the illustrations herald the blend of all these elements which was to mark the establishment of true Byzantine art. Constantinople seems the most likely place in which the mingling of influences that we see here would have taken place. The manuscript has been dated to the fourth, fifth and sixth centuries by different investigators. On the whole a date shortly before 500 seems most probable—the blending of styles has gone too far for the fourth century, and it is not yet complete enough for the full sixth, certainly if the attribution to Constantinople is correct. The Genesis would seem, however, to belong to an earlier phase than the Rossano Codex.

The illuminations of this fine manuscript are on a more monumental scale. They occupy larger portions of each page, and approach in character the single-page illustrations which became almost universal at a later date, rather than the inter-

---

[1] "Notes on East Christian Miniatures", *Art Bulletin*, XI, 1929, p. 12. See also H. Gerstinger, *Die Wiener Genesis*, Vienna, 1931, for a full publication with excellent coloured plates.

polations in the text which were typical earlier. Portraits of the Evangelists were included before each Gospel, and the iconography of the New Testament scenes was fully developed; some of them constitute quite fine pictures. The Entry into Jerusalem is thus an impressive composition and shows the iconography of the scene in a fully developed form (*Byzantine Art*, pl. 27); the Raising of Lazarus is both profound and moving (Pl. 14, *b*). Large heads, rather theatrical gestures and a somewhat pattern-like arrangement of the figures attests the eastern element in these miniatures, and Christ is conceived as the dark-haired, bearded figure of eastern iconography. But the fusion of styles is on the whole more complete than in the Vienna Genesis, and if the manuscript was indeed illuminated at Constantinople, a date shortly before the middle of the sixth century seems most likely. But the provenance is not certain, and Morey has made out a good case for assigning both manuscripts to Asia Minor.[1]

The orientalising style of most of these religious manuscripts may be contrasted with that of the majority of the illustrations of the few secular ones that survive. True, one copy of Virgil in the Vatican, the Codex Romanus, is in a rather "expressionist" manner, but a second and more important one is completely Pompeian,[2] and an Iliad in the Ambrosian Library at Milan is again primarily classical, though there are Byzantine elements in its style. The Virgils are probably to be assigned to the fifth century; the Iliad may even belong to the sixth.[3] Another important secular manuscript is the Dioscorides at Vienna which has already been mentioned. Its style is rather more Latin, anyhow so far as the title page is concerned, which bears the portrait of Julia Anicia, sister of Honorius, between two personifications. The manuscript was done at Constantinople shortly before 512. This illumination, when considered alongside the silver plates in the Hermitage, serves to show that the secular art was much less orientalised than the religious, and proves that the changes of style came about as a direct result of the establishment and adoption of the new faith, and not

---

[1] "Sources of Mediaeval Art", *Art Bulletin*, VII, 1929, pp. 37, 42. For a full publication with coloured plates see A. Munoz, *Il Codice Purpureo di Rossano*, Rome, 1907.

[2] Numbers 3867 and 3225 respectively. Both are fully published in the Vatican series of facsimiles, vols. II and I.

[3] It has recently been fully and admirably published by R. B. Bandinelli, *Hellenistic-Byzantine Miniatures of the Iliad*, Olten, 1955. See especially ch. V.

because of progressive decadence of classical art, as some critics have held. The new ideas must have penetrated the lower ranks of society first, while the aristocracy remained on the whole more conservative.

Of all the cities of the Byzantine empire, Salonica was probably most closely allied to Constantinople, and the works that were done there probably reflect very closely the ideas and styles of the capital. Luckily several buildings of early date with vestiges of mosaic decorations survive there, and in default of examples at Constantinople we may turn to these to complete our picture. The earliest of them is the mosaic decoration of the round church of St. George. In the vaults of the chambers that project from the central circle the decoration is aniconic, but of very high quality; the mosaics are perhaps more closely comparable to those of the aisle vaults in Sta Constanza or the Lateran Baptistry at Rome than to any others. More impressive, however, in spite of its fragmentary state, is the decoration at the summit of the great dome above. At the centre was a representation of Christ triumphant before a great mandorla or "glory", upheld by four archangels. Lower down, at the spring of the dome, was a vast "architecturescape", with figures of martyrs isolated in front of it (Pl. 16, *a*). It is not dissimilar from the decoration of the Orthodox Baptistry at Ravenna, but it is on a larger scale and the style is colder and more severe; it is in fact more purely "neo-Attic". One would on stylistic grounds alone suggest a somewhat earlier date than that of the earliest work at Ravenna (*c.* 440), and a very good case has recently been made out for assigning it to the days of Theodosios the Great (379-395).[1] It is a tragedy that so little of these very fine mosaics is preserved.

Though only decorative work in the spandrels of the arches survives, the mosaics of the great basilica once called Sta Paraskevi, but now known as the Panaghia Achieropoietou, are of equally high quality. They must belong to a slightly later date—say to the early fifth century. The scrolls and the selection of fruits and flowers that form the repertory of these mosaics is unusually rich. In a rather different style, but equally fine from the artistic point of view, is a composition in the apse—all that remains—of a church higher up the hill, known variously as

[1] H. Torp, "Les Mosaïques de St. Georges à Thessalonique", *Proceedings of IX Byzantine Congress at Salonica*, Athens, 1955, p. 491.

Hosios David or the Panaghia tou Latomou (Our Lady of the stone mason). It shows the Vision of Ezechiel; Christ, beardless, and youthful, is enthroned on an arc, before a circular glory from behind which appear the four apocalyptic beasts. To His right is a diminutive figure of the prophet, to His left a similar figure representing Habakkuk. The style is less "neo-Attic" than at St. George's and the mosaic may be compared with those in the apses of Sta Constanza at Rome. Like them, it is to be dated to the fifth century.

All these mosaics are of extremely high quality and represent the best work of their age. A few others, rather farther afield, are more provincial in style, notably those in the apse of the church of the monastery of St. Catherine on Mount Sinai, where the Transfiguration is shown as a large figural composition. The monastery was founded between 548 and 562, but the Prior mentioned in an inscription on the mosaic was appointed rather later. He was alive when the mosaic was done, for he appears in it with the square nimbus always associated with the living. The date that tallies best with these and other factors is 565, and the mosaic must have been set up soon after that year.[1]

To the later sixth or early seventh century again belongs an apse mosaic at Chiti in Cyprus, which shows the Virgin, full length and holding the Child, between two winged angels (Pl. 17). The Virgin is tall and dignified, the angels move towards her with a fine swinging movement. The work is provincial like that at Sinai, but recent cleaning has shown it to be of far higher quality than was at one time supposed. The decorative work at the side of the panel, for example, is particularly effective. An interesting fact is that the Virgin is here designated as "St. Mary", a designation usual in Coptic Egypt, where her role as the "Mother of God" was not admitted. In another mosaic in Cyprus, at Lythrangomi, she is shown before a glory of brilliant colour, the object of which was no doubt to stress the conception of her divinity.[2]

It has sometimes been held that Justinian left the country so exhausted and the treasury so depleted at his death that no further work under imperial patronage was possible for a

---

[1] Benesvrić, "Date de la mosaïque du Mont Sinai", *Byzantion*, I, 1924, p. 145.
[2] See an interesting article by A. Grabar in *Studies in Honor of A. M. Friend*, Princeton, 1955.

century or more. Like many statements, inspired probably by Gibbon's conception of the steady decline of the east Roman empire, this interpretation is far from correct. As Dr. Underwood has shown, Justinian's successor, Justin II, set up mosaics in Sancta Sophia; he and many of his successors built extensively in the Great Palace at Constantinople; many of them founded churches there and elsewhere, and individual patrons were rich enough to undertake considerable activities on their own. And if we know but little of the arts of the centuries between Justinian's death (565) and the beginnings of Iconoclasm (726), it is not so much because nothing was done as because little has survived. But recent research is beginning to fill the gap, and two series of mosaics in the east Christian world can now be assigned with reasonable certainty to the age following Justinian, namely those of St. Demetrius at Salonica and some of the earliest of the work in the church of the Assumption at Nicaea. The latter was wantonly destroyed about 1920; the former was burnt accidentally in 1917, but happily only some of the mosaics perished, and additional ones on the piers of the nave were then discovered as a result of the fire.

The mosaics of St. Demetrius, the earliest of which are probably to be dated to the late sixth century, fall into rather a different category from those of other churches, for though there are to-day as many as eight distinct panels on the piers, and before the fire there were also eight subjects on the nave walls, all of them were of a votive character, and each contained a figure of the patron saint. They must have been set up at intervals throughout the sixth, seventh and probably also the early eighth centuries; it is hardly likely that any were erected during Iconoclasm (726-843), nor would the style accord with so late a date.

The earliest of these panels is probably that which has been most often reproduced, which shows St. Demetrius between two donors whose square haloes denote their sanctity and also the fact that they were still living when the mosaic was set up (*Byzantine Art*, pl. 9). Technically the work is of a very high quality, and stylistically it shows a complete fusion of the ideas and elements which went to make up Byzantine art. The costume of the secular donor is thus basically classical, and his face is an obvious portrait; the bishop's robe is shown in a more

(a) Ivory. Joshua receiving envoys from the people of Gibeon. Probably tenth century. (*Photo Victoria and Albert Museum.*)

PLATE 15

(b) The Joshua Roll. The same scene as above. *c.* 700. (*Photo Vatican Library.*)

(*a*) Salonica. St. George. Dome mosaic. Perhaps late fourth century.
(*Photo Dyggve.*)

(*b*) Damascus. The Great Mosque. Detail of mosaic. 715. (*Photo de Lorey.*)

PLATE 16

B. Salonica. St. Demetrius. Mosaic. Seventh century. (*Photo Powell.*)

formal manner, and the high-lights on his face are more abstract, as becomes a dignitary of the church; the Saint, youthful, but of an essentially other-worldly hierarchy, stands between them, as if levitated above the earth. The art is expressive and interpretational, but at the same time has a dignity combined with a decorative charm, which is characteristic of the best Byzantine work. Other compositions in the church are similar; some have a greater profusion of detail, and scenes of this world, like a delightful garden with a fountain in it, play a prominent part; others are rather less proficient technically; some again are well nigh as fine as the first panel we have noted, like one showing St. Demetrius and two children (Pl. B). To put them into an exact chronological series is not easy, but stylistic developments are clear and certain repairs could be distinguished in the destroyed work which originally decorated the nave arcades.

The loss of the mosaics of the church of the Assumption of the Virgin at Nicaea is one of the great tragedies of recent times, for they must have been of really outstanding quality. Nicaea was near to Constantinople geographically and must always have been in close contact with the city; it was as well an important centre of ecclesiastical thought. One would have expected to find there work of the highest quality, but work also which tended to reflect the outlook of the leading ecclesiastics of the day rather than that of the court. The decoration that survived until about 1920 belonged to a number of different periods; the earliest mosaics, represented by four figures of archangels on the vault before the apse, was probably done in the seventh century. The angels, who are called Arche, Dynamis, Kyriotites and Exonsie, are in imperial costume and each holds a banner or long staff in one hand and an orb in the other. They are grand and impressive, but the true glory of this work is to be seen in the detail of the heads (Pl. 20, *a*). The modelling is effective, and the palette must have been very rich, but it is the curious, aloof yet gentle expression of the faces that is particularly moving; it moves one almost to tears when one thinks that they were there, to be seen, only so short a time ago.[1]

[1] G. de Francovich has recently suggested that these mosaics should be assigned to the sixth century; see "I Mosaici del bema della chiesa della dormizione di Nicaea " in *Scritti in Onore di Lionello Venturi*, Rome, 1956.

G

If the Nicaean work is impressive for what may be termed its humanistic quality, two other series of mosaics, this time exactly dated, are equally so as pieces of glorious decoration. They are those in the Dome of the Rock at Jerusalem (691-692) and the Great Mosque at Damascus (715), both done for Islamic patrons, though in an essentially Byzantine style. The work in the Dome of the Rock, consisting of scrolls, candelabra motifs and so on, is pure decoration. That at Damascus, with its lovely trees, its delightful hill towns, and its enchantingly fantastic architectural compositions (Pl. 16, *b*), represents a grand example of the survival of the old "picturesque" and "architecturescape" styles. Perspective plays a much smaller part here than it did in so much of the work at Pompeii, but there is a new fantasy, a new delight in decoration for its own sake, which seems to herald the taste of a Rex Whistler. Though done for an Islamic Caliph, the genesis of the work, through such steps as St. George at Salonica or the Baptistry of the Orthodox at Ravenna, is clear. Tradition has it that artists were brought from Constantinople to help with the work, and even if Miss Van Berchem is right when she asserts that there is much that is Syrian about it,[1] it is tempting to accept the legend on its face value and to suggest that a few at least of the mosaicists, and probably the chief master himself, came from the Byzantine capital. It is a perfect piece of Iconoclast art; and it may be suggested that quite a lot of work of this type was done at Constantinople during the next century when representational compositions were forbidden by the dictates of the Iconoclast emperors. But nothing survives, and it is with the delights of Damascus fresh in our minds that we should pass to the next phase of Byzantine art, which began anew after the end of Iconoclasm, rather than by way of Italy and the rather arid work that was done there throughout the later eighth and the ninth centuries.

BOOKS

L. Bréhier, *La Sculpture et les arts mineurs byzantins*, Paris, 1936.

Ch. Diehl, M. le Tourneau and H. Saladin, *Les Monuments chrétiens de Salonique*, Paris, 1918.

[1] In K. A. C. Creswell, *Early Muslim Architecture*, I, p. 251.

CHAPTER VII

THE EIGHTH CENTURY IN THE EAST
AND PROBLEMS OF DATING

MOREY has put forward the ingenious suggestion that as a result of the Islamic conquest of Egypt around 645, artists fled the city and eventually established themselves in various places in the Christian world. He suggests that Hosios David at Salonica was the work of one of them, but this contention can no longer be allowed, for the mosaics are certainly very much earlier—as stated above, they are probably to be assigned to the fifth century (p. 95)—nor are they sufficiently Alexandrine in style to justify such a supposition. Next, he attributes certain of the paintings in Sta Maria Antiqua to Alexandrian artists, and this suggestion is more plausible, for the wall paintings there undoubtedly show a great intermingling of styles and influences, and some among them are very Hellenistic.[1] Other painters went perhaps to Constantinople and others to the West, where they laid the foundations on which Carolingian art was built. The lovely frescoes of Castelseprio near Milan are, thinks Morey, to be attributed to one of these Alexandrine painters who found his way to northern Italy.

This is, however, all very problematic. What is far more important is that manuscripts done in Alexandria and based on the original Septuagint illustrations found their way to other places and were copied, sometimes faithfully, sometimes with variations, and sometimes on a large as well as on a small scale. In judging these copies, it is essential to take into account both the personal style of the copyist and the influence of the place in which he worked, in addition to the nature of the original. Naturally, it is in iconography that the original shows its influence most obviously, but at times even the style survived through that of the later copying in great purity. Such is the case with what is the most important of the manuscripts of this

---

[1] M. Avery, "The Alexandrian Style at Santa Maria Antiqua", *Art Bulletin*, VII, 1925, p. 131.

age, the Roll of Joshua in the Vatican library (*Byzantine Art*, pl. 28).

Of recent years a great deal of argument has raged as to the actual date of this manuscript. Morey would assign it to about 700, and describes it as "a perfect example of the continuous method", a system which was probably important in early times, when the roll was in more general favour than the paged book. It reproduces, almost exactly he thinks, a Pentateuch illustration of the second century which was also in the form of a roll.[1] Many others agree with this conclusion, though they are less definite in their estimation of the date, the fifth, sixth and seventh centuries having all been suggested. Weitzmann on the other hand puts the existing manuscript as late as the tenth century, looking upon it as an archaicising work, due to the antiquarian tastes of the Emperor Constantine Porphyrogenitus (913-949), and he also believes that it was not modelled on a roll, but on a leaved book, bridge pieces being subsequently put in to produce the continuous effect. He thinks that this book was very similar to the original from which the twelfth century Octateuchs were copied; these represent another instance of the use of Alexandrine Septuagint models in later times.[2] None of the Octateuchs are, however, earlier than the twelfth century, and even if they reproduce the iconography of the Alexandrine Septuagint, their style is completely distinct. Many of the scenes that appear in the Octateuchs are, however, the same as those in the Joshua Rotulus, and they can be used as guides to fill in lacunae where they exist at the ends of the roll. But the comparison of the Octateuchs hardly supports Weitzmann's conclusion as to date, for their style is so very different from that of the Rotulus.

Weitzmann's thesis is extremely well presented, with a wealth of evidence, but it is not wholly convincing, either with regard to date or to the copying of a paginated original rather than a roll, and Morey's arguments, on the whole, seem the more convincing. This being so, an ivory in the Victoria and Albert Museum showing Joshua receiving envoys, which is wellnigh identical with the rendering of the same scene in the Rotulus, is also perhaps to be assigned to the seventh rather

[1] *Mediaeval Art*, p. 50; *Early Christian Art*, p. 69; "Notes on East Christian Miniatures", *Art Bulletin*, XI, 1929, pp. 48 ff.

[2] *Illustrations in Roll and Codex*, Princeton, 1947, and *The Joshua Roll*, Princeton, 1948, *passim*.

than the tenth century though on the whole the later date is
more likely. (Pl. 15); it is especially interesting as proof of
the close inter-relation between the various arts in the Byzantine
world. But certain other conclusions which Weitzmann reaches
are more generally acceptable, notably with regard to the
tenth century date of an important group of ivories with classi-
cising scenes, which had previously sometimes been assigned to
the Iconoclast period. They all form parts of caskets, known
as the Rosette caskets; the finest of all is that known as the
Veroli casket in the Victoria and Albert Museum.

Weitzmann's case for dating another important manuscript,
known as the Paris Psalter (Bib. Nat. Gr. 139), to the tenth
century is far better substantiated than that for the Rotulus.
This manuscript consists of a text which is certainly of the
tenth century, with fourteen illustrations on leaves of a different
parchment from the text; they may perhaps be interpolations.
Five hands can be distinguished in these illustrations; one of
them was a master of great ability, with a very fine feeling for
colour, and a good sense of movement; he favoured perspective
backgrounds and loved personifications. He was responsible,
amongst others, for the scenes showing David composing the
Psalms (*Byzantine Art*, pl. 30) and the Prophecy of Isaiah (Pl.
18).[1] In the former, the landscape setting, the picturesque treatment of the animals, still reminiscent of an Orpheus scene, and
the personification of Melodia behind David all show the close-
ness with which an Alexandrine model must have been
followed. In the latter, Isaiah stands between Night and Dawn
against a very effective background of foliage. Night, as a tall
female figure of Hellenistic type with a veil over her head, is
especially impressive. So Hellenistic are the illustrations that
Morey suggests that an Alexandrine roll was the ultimate
model; the actual illustrations were, however, done in Constantinople. He argues for a date before Iconoclasm, though he
thinks that this manuscript may have been done rather later
than the Rotulus. But in reaching this conclusion he does not

[1] He also did David slaying the Lion, the Crossing of the Red Sea, Moses on
Sinai, and the Prayer of Hezekiah. Of the other hands one, an inadequate follower
of the master, did the Combat of David and Goliath and the Anointing of David;
one, a very incompetent artist, did the Daughters of Israel and David, and the
Coronation of David; and another, who favoured very static poses, did the
Exaltation of David and David's Penitence. The fifth artist, whose style was more
oriental, did the story of Jonah and Hannah's prayer. See C. R. Morey, "Notes
on East Christian Miniatures", *Art Bulletin*, XI, 1929, pp. 3-30.

take into full account the very close similarity between the illustrations of the Paris Psalter and some in another manuscript in the Bibliothèque Nationale (Gr. 510), the Homilies of Gregory Nazianzus, which was done for Basil I and is thus firmly dated to between 880 and 886.

This manuscript contains a mass of full-page illustrations, in a number of different manners. Some show crowded scenes rather like those in the Cappadocian wall paintings (see p. 107); others are aniconic and consist of a decorative leaved cross, savouring of the tastes of Iconoclast times[1]; others again have lovely full-page compositions, like that bearing the vision of the Prophet Ezechiel (Pl. 19). Such illustrations as this are obviously closely akin to those of the Paris Psalter, and if the one series could have been done in the ninth century, there is every reason to suppose that the other was done also. More-over, the style of these miniatures, in brilliant and very effective colours, is what Wölfflin would have called "painterly", whereas that of the Joshua Roll is essentially "linear"[2]; its illustrations are in fact no more than tinted drawings, so that the two are really hardly comparable at all. And again, if the twelfth century Octateuchs can reproduce early Alexandrine models as faithfully as they do, surely the painter of the Paris Psalter could reproduce them in the ninth century? A dating in the ninth or early tenth century is also supported by the similarity of the Psalter miniatures to those of a manuscript in the Vatican (Reg. Gr. 1) which was done for the Patrician Leo in the second quarter of the tenth century.

There are a number of other manuscripts that are more or less closely related to the Homilies of Gregory Nazianzus (Paris, Gr. 510), but they are all of definitely post-Iconoclast date and are essentially Byzantine works rather than Alex-andrine survivals—as indeed are most of the miniatures of the Homilies itself. They will be considered in due course; the Homilies had to be mentioned here because of its bearing on the problems of dating the Rotulus and the Paris Psalter. The same is true of the Octateuchs; a study of their iconography may have much to tell us about Septuagint art, but their style is typical

---

[1] G. Millet, "Les Iconoclastes et la Croix", *Bulletin de Correspondance hellénique*, XXXIV, 1910, p. 96; D. Talbot Rice, "The Leaved Cross", in *Byzantino-slavica*, XI, Prague, 1950, p. 72.

[2] For a definition of these terms see Wölfflin, *Principles of Art History*, London, 1932.

of all that the Second Golden Age of Byzantine art stood for.

There is, however, one other very important monument which is probably to be dated to pre-Iconoclast times, namely the frescoed decoration in the small church at Castelseprio, near Milan, which was discovered as short a time ago as 1944. The frescoes are in a style that owes a lot to the Hellenistic world and represent scenes from the life of the Virgin and the infancy of Christ. They occupy two zones in the apse; below them is a third zone, bearing decorative compositions. All are battered—indeed the lowest zone is almost entirely destroyed—but enough survives to attest the very high quality of the work. The scenes comprise the Annunciation to the Virgin, the Visitation, the Proof of the Virgin, Joseph's Dream, the Journey to Bethlehem, the Nativity and the Annunciation to the Shepherds (Pl. 21, a), the Adoration, and the Presentation in the Temple.

The very high quality of these paintings was realised as soon as they were discovered, and they are now generally accepted as one of the really outstanding monuments of early Christian art. But once more the date is debated, as is also the school to which they should be assigned. The discoverers thus favoured a date in the seventh century, and suggested that the paintings were done by an artist from Syria; the mosaics of Sinai and certain of the paintings of Kusejr Amra (c. 711) were cited as proof of the high standard of work in that area.[1] Morey preferred one around 700, but attributed the work to an Alexandrine artist—one of those driven out by the Islamic conquest around 640. He cited paintings in Sta Maria Antiqua at Rome as parallel instances of this Alexandrine influence.[2] Weitzmann, on the other hand, compared the paintings to the Joshua Rotulus and dated them, along with it and the Paris Psalter (Paris, Gr. 139), to the ninth or tenth century. He also attributed the work to a Constantinopolitan painter. He supported his conclusions by noting amongst other things that there were very close relationships between Hugo of Arles, King of Italy (926-941), and the Byzantine capital,[3] and

[1] G. P. Bognetti, G. Chierici and A. de Capetani d'Arzago, *Santa Maria di Castelseprio*, Milan, 1948.
[2] C. R. Morey, "Castelseprio and the Byzantine Renaissance", *Art Bulletin*, XXXIV, 1952.
[3] K. Weitzmann, *The Fresco Cycle of S. Maria di Castelseprio*, Princeton, 1951.

suggested that the work was done under Hugo's patronage. Grabar thought the paintings had a distinctly western flavour, and assigned them to late Carolingian or early Ottonian art.[1]

There are a few definite facts that bear on the question of dating. Thus there are graffiti scratched on the paintings which mention the name of Andericus, who was Archbishop of Milan from 938 to 945; the paintings must thus be earlier than 945. One would assume that they would be considerably earlier, for one would hardly expect to find such mutilation taking place while the paintings were still comparatively new. Other graffiti suggest a date before 868, but their evidence is not final. Conclusions on archaeological or epigraphical evidence are thus indefinite. But some time has now elapsed since the paintings were discovered, time enough in any case for ideas to crystalise, and the general consensus of opinion supports the earlier dating rather than that of Weitzmann.

With regard to style, there is less conformity of opinion. Few, indeed, would support Capetani d'Arzago's suggestion that the artist was a Syrian. Antioch had been destroyed by an earthquake in 526 and the city had never really recovered from the shock. Islam had dominated the region since before the middle of the seventh century, and the picture of Syrian art available to us does not support the claim that work of such elegance and delicacy as that at Castelseprio was produced there, even when Christian Syria was most prosperous. As Weitzmann points out, the Sinai mosaics show a good deal of Constantinopolitan influence, and the Kusejr Amra frescoes are far from typical; some, it is true, are delicate and essentially Hellenistic, but others, notably the portraits of kings overcome by Islam, are in the essentially eastern style which is to be seen at an earlier date at Palmyra and Dura. The work was done for an Islamic patron in the eighth century.[2] Morey's theory of Alexandrine emigration is attractive, but there is little concrete evidence to support it; indeed, there is actually no single work of art which can be definitely assigned to Alexandria; all the attributions rest upon hypotheses, often very ingenious, but not necessarily reliable.

[1] "Les Fresques de Castelseprio et l'Occident", in *Frühmittelalterliche Kunst in den Alpenländern, Actes du III Congrès International pour l'étude du haut moyen âge*, Olten-Lausanne, 1954, p. 85.
[2] The best reproductions are those in K. A. C. Creswell, *Early Muslim Architecture*, Vol. I, Oxford, 1932.

Chiti, Cyprus. The Virgin between the Archangels Michael and Gabriel.
Late sixth century. (*Photo Dept. of Antiquities, Cyprus.*)

PLATE 17

The Paris Psalter (Bib. Nat. Gr. 139): the Prophecy of Isaiah.
Probably tenth century. (*Photo Bibliothèque Nationale.*)

PLATE 18

The Homilies of Gregory Nazianzus (Bib. Nat. Gr. 510): the Vision
of the Prophet Ezechiel.   880-886.   (*Photo Bibliothèque Nationale.*)

PLATE 19

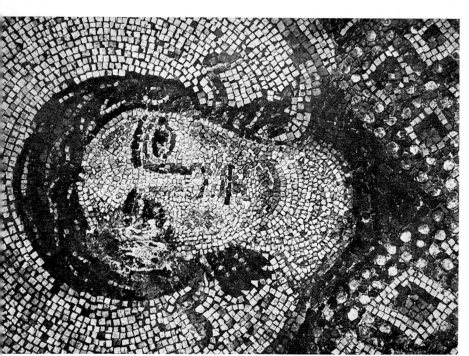

PLATE 20

(a) Head of Archangel. Seventh century.

(b) Virgin in the Apse. Detail. Ninth century.

Nicaea. Church of the Assumption of the Virgin.

(*Both after Schmidt.*)

With regard to Constantinople, on the other hand, we do know something rather more definite, thanks to the mosaics of the Great Palace, the silver work, and the sculptures in the Museum of Antiquities. The most relevant of these are probably those on the Panachrantos arch (Fig. 11). Here, alas, the date has again been disputed, though the sixth century is more likely than the tenth. But two facts stand out—the arch was sculptured in Constantinople, and it shows work of the same delicacy and high quality as that at Castelseprio. It is admittedly not easy to arrive at conclusions as to the school to which paintings should be assigned by studying sculpture, but this comparison is suggestive. Further, there are certain relationships between Castelseprio and the eleventh century paintings in Sancta Sophia at Ochrid in Yugoslavia, which were undoubtedly done under Constantinopolitan influence. The relationships are to be seen especially in the faces, with their curiously pinched-in noses and marked cheek bones—the figure of Joseph in the scene of the Proof of the Virgin at Castelseprio may be compared with that of Abraham in the scene of his sacrifice in Sancta Sophia at Ochrid.[1] The resemblances here do not necessarily suggest a closely similar date, but they do attest an identical heritage, and that heritage must clearly have been a Constantinopolitan one. Other evidence that favours a Constantinopolitan provenance for the art has been put forward by Weitzmann. On the whole, therefore, there seem good grounds to associate the Castelseprio paintings primarily with Constantinople. As to date, the later part of the eighth century seems most likely; though earlier in the eighth is not impossible; it may even be that artists left Constantinople at the beginning of Iconoclasm (726) and sought commissions elsewhere in the way that Morey suggests that they left Alexandria at a rather earlier date. If so, the Castelseprio paintings might well have been done by one of them.

Whatever their heritage, however, the Castelseprio paintings stand somewhat apart, and in an opposite direction they would seem to be just as closely related to works of a primarily western character, like the Utrecht Psalter (see p. 126), as they are to Byzantine ones, and they occupy just as important a place in the history of Carolingian art as they do in that of Byzantine. We shall thus have cause to refer to them again in the third part

[1] For an excellent colour plate of this see *Yugoslavia: Mediaeval Frescoes*, Unesco World Art Series, 1955, pl. 3.

of this book. Indeed, in some ways they are closer to the works done in the West after 900 than to those done in the East, just because the West was on the whole more conservative and remained faithful to classical models for a longer time than did Byzantium, where a new and very distinctive style was developing from the end of the tenth century onwards as the result of the penetration of eastern ideas.

The first developments of this mid-Byzantine style are to be traced in manuscripts rather than in works on a major scale. One of the most important is that known as the Leningrad Lectionary. It occupies an important place in the story of Byzantine art, for its numerous miniatures, though they savour in many ways of Syria, have also something of the majestic quality that characterises the best and most typically Constantinopolitan work. They show clearly the influence of such a grand and sophisticated manuscript as the Rossanensis in the one direction, and in the other show the eastern style that was to culminate in the Cappadocian wall paintings (see p. 107). The manuscript is probably to be dated to the eighth century, and Morey makes out a very good case for assigning it to Asia Minor, to the same area as he attributes the Vienna Genesis and the Rossano Codex.[1]

A series of rather similar miniatures are preserved in another manuscript, the Etchmiadzin Gospels. Their date has been disputed. There are ten leaves with illustrations, bound up with an Armenian text dated to 989, and it was at one time held that the illustrations had been re-used and were actually to be assigned to the seventh century and attributed to Syria. The most recent view is that they belong to the same date as the text. Most of the miniatures are enclosed in arcaded frames like those of the canon tables of the Rabula manuscript, and they must have been modelled upon these. The paintings are not all by the same hand, but all are in an essentially eastern style.

A few eastern works on a larger scale also fall for consideration here, notably some of the earlier of the wall paintings in the rock-cut churches of Cappadocia and those in caves near Miletus at a place called Latmos. Both series are primitive and represent a localised monastic art, the products of which it is

---

[1] "Notes on East Christian Manuscripts", *Art Bulletin*, XI, 1929, especially pp. 90 ff.

by no means easy to date. The Latmos paintings may, however, be as early as the eighth century, and they are certainly
not later than the eleventh. Those in the rock-cut churches of
Cappadocia can be more definitely dated, both on external and
on stylistic grounds. Some are as late as the eleventh century,
but others are earlier and were no doubt done during Iconoclasm, for the ban on religious art was never effectually
exercised in out-of-the-way regions, especially in monastic
circles, where the theological ideas behind the ban were always
disputed.

The iconography of the Cappadocian paintings is important,
for it shows us a wide extension of the themes known from the
earlier eastern models, and it is on the evidence afforded by
Cappadocia that many of our conclusions as to the nature of
eastern style as well as eastern iconography have to be founded.
All sorts of rather unusual and obscure themes were favoured
there owing to the monastic and hence theologically inclined
outlook of the society for which the paintings were done, namely
the monks and hermits who inhabited the numerous cells in the
region and used the chapels and churches. Scenes were usually
crowded together with the object of including as much as
possible of the story on the walls of each chapel, so that the
general effect is rather confused. The work, too, was often
rather primitive and the colours strange and quite non-
naturalistic. But they were well chosen and the paintings have
at worst a vividness and sincerity, at best a deep power of
expression, which makes them far from negligible as works
of art. A portrayal of Christ in the dome of the Church at
Elmale Kilisse may serve as an example (Pl. 21, b); it dates
from the twelfth century. The stylised rhythms of the angels
are effective, and there is a profound reverence about the
whole picture.

A series of rather similar "monastic" paintings also exists in
cave chapels in the region of Bari in southern Italy, and there
were doubtless links between the two regions, for southern Italy
was still essentially Byzantine in culture at this date and
churches survive there which are completely Byzantine so far
as their architecture is concerned. But these paintings represent
a side line or offshoot in the story of Christian art, whereas
Cappadocia was a source of inspiration elsewhere: the region
cannot indeed be passed by even in a study which is primarily

concerned with the aesthetic quality of the paintings. There will be frequent cause to refer to this school, especially in connection with certain of the eleventh century mosaics of Greece and later paintings in the Balkans, which owed a great deal, both stylistically and iconographically, to the more primitive art of Asia Minor.

BOOKS

G. DE JERPLIANION, *Les Eglises rupestres de la Cappadoce*, Paris, 1925-42.

K. WEITZMANN, *Illustrations in Roll and Codex*, Princeton, 1947; *The Joshua Roll*, 1948; *The Fresco Cycle of S. Maria di Castelseprio*, 1951.

Part III

DEVELOPMENTS IN THE WEST

From the early eighth century developments in the East, which depended on the new capital at Constantinople, and in the West, which looked towards Rome, began to follow distinctive lines. In the East they were profoundly affected by the puritan outlook of Iconoclasm; in the West the patronage of the Popes was responsible for a good deal of figural work, though some of it would seem to have been done with political rather than artistic ends in view. The work thus lacks the brilliance and fervent religious emotion of that done just after Iconoclasm in the East, but it is, none the less, interesting. With the coronation of Charlemagne as emperor of the West in 800 the independence of the path of development in the West was accentuated, and though there were undoubtedly frequent interchanges of styles and ideas between East and West, Carolingian artists on the whole preferred to look back to early Christian or even classical models, so that their art was more conservative than that produced in the East. Much was done in Italy, especially under the patronage of the Popes and later under that of Benedictine monasticism, but as the centre of power was at Aachen in western Germany, it was there and thereabouts that the most important developments took place. The Carolingian phase in northern Europe gave way to the Ottonian soon after 900. One of the Ottos, after whom the new dynasty was called, married a Byzantine princess, and in the third quarter of the tenth century Aachen was being modelled on Constantinople. But though Byzantine influence was much more marked than in the Carolingian age, Ottonian art was nevertheless distinctive, and paved the way for the development of the new phase we know as Romanesque soon after the year 1000. At one time the great aesthetic quality of this phase was ignored, but to-day its genius is universally admired. Monuments in architecture and sculpture, and to some extent in painting also, are, however, very numerous and the style is so important that space does not permit of its treatment here.

The early art of Britain constitutes a chapter somewhat apart, for it developed along its own lines, first in Northumbria and Ireland, and later in Saxon Wessex. But in early times the influence of the early Christian art of the Mediterranean world was fundamental, and in later times there were important links with the Continent north of the Alps, and at times these even extended to the Byzantine world.

CHAPTER VIII

PAINTING IN ITALY FROM THE EIGHTH TO THE TWELFTH CENTURY

WHILE all these developments were taking place in the East, Italy was not completely stagnant, though work done there was not only a good deal less lavish, owing to the absence of imperial patronage, but also less inspiring. The Hellenistic and eastern elements which had played an important part in the formation of Byzantine art were absent, and in many ways what was done in Italy represented a decline rather than a renewal; that is to say the subject matter changed, being Christian, but the style remained provincial and the quality fairly low. Nor was the same overriding religious enthusiasm present, for paganism subsisted longer in the West than in the East, and the fervent influence of monasticism was absent, for it was in Egypt and Syria that this aspect of the new faith flourished most markedly. In fact, what was done in Italy after the decline of the great cities like Rome, Milan and Ravenna was of secondary quality and of local rather than universal importance. The best work was that done under the patronage of the Popes, and for practically the whole of the period with which we are dealing in this chapter it was in Rome itself and under the auspices of the Popes that the most active production took place. Only towards its close did the patronage of monastic orders, more especially that of the Benedictines, begin to play a similarly important part.

Something has already been said of the mosaics set up in a number of Roman churches at this time. They represent the richest work in point of material, but though the colours are effective and some of the work, especially that in the chapel of St. Zeno in Sta Praxede, is really fine, much of it is rather monotonous and wooden, and lacks movement and life in comparison with what was done in the East. A word has also been said about the paintings of Sta Maria Antiqua in the Forum, but they deserve further consideration, for some are of great quality. Four separate styles are to be distinguished in these paintings. Some are distinctly eastern, and show features of Syrian origin, like the colobium or long robe worn by Christ in the Crucifixion scene, in place of the Byzantine loin cloth. Some would appear to have been inspired from Alexandria, and show a distinctly classical outlook, like the angel whose elegant form is so very distinctive (Pl. 40, *a*). Some of these paintings were clearly inspired by Byzantine, perhaps even Constantinopolitan art, for example the St. Andrew (*Byzantine Art*, pl. 15), where high-lights are slashed on in a manner suggestive of the later mosaics and paintings. Finally, some of the paintings are essentially Italianate. This manner is well illustrated by such compositions as the enthroned Virgin or the Christ, where the figures are posed severely and frontally, with inscriptions arranged formally on either side of the heads, as in Byzantine work. But the heads are large and the proportions inelegant, and the whole rendering is rather primitive and arid. It is this last manner that concerns us in this chapter, for it was widely spread over Italy by the ninth century, by which date it had developed into a distinctively Italian style.

The characteristics that distinguish it in its developed form are fairly clear; in addition to the large heads and inelegant proportions, the expressions are set and staring, the eyes large, the figures rigid, the poses severe and the general effect rather wooden. Above all, the work somehow lacks the transcendental outlook of the fully fledged Byzantine, as well as the emotional character of the Syrian. It tells its story effectively, however, and in this respect attests the heritage from classical Rome, where narrative was always important. But the story is told in prose rather than in verse, with the aim of recording to the fore, rather than that of inspiring, as was the case in the Byzantine world. But even if much of the work is rather clumsy, every now and again it reached to really great heights, notably in a panel of the Virgin, now in the church of Sta Maria Novella at Rome, which was only recently disclosed by the removal of a mass of later overpainting (Pl. C). The panel is quite large, and the painting carefully and subtly modelled, and the tones merge gently one into the other; the characteristic Byzantine high-lights are completely absent. Especially noteworthy are the delicate pink tones of the flesh, laid over a green undercoat, and the almond-shaped eyes with eyebrows curling over them

C. Rome. Sta Maria Novella. Panel. Seventh century. (*Photo Powell.*)

like hooks and forming a continuous line with the shadow of the nose. The date of the panel has been disputed, for some would assign it to as early as the fifth century, whereas Kitzinger, in a recent publication, has put forward evidence in favour of the seventh.[1] The similar approach of the painter to that of the man responsible for some of the work in Sta Maria Antiqua, which must be dated to the eighth century, supports the later dating.

By no means all the work done in Italy in the seventh, eighth and ninth centuries was, however, of such high quality, and the wall paintings as a whole are a great deal more pedestrian. But even if this is so, all the work is nevertheless interesting, and shows the development of new stylistic ideas and new iconographical themes. Some of the most important of them are paintings which survive below the church of San Clemente. They are of various dates, the best of them being earlier than the present basilica, which was rebuilt after the destruction of its predecessor by the Normans in 1084. Most important is a series of paintings of the life of Christ done under the patronage of Pope Leo IV (847-855). The Crucifixion and the Ascension may be noted (Pl. 22, a). In the latter the Pope is shown at one end of the composition, with a square halo behind his head, denoting that he was still living when the work was done. At the opposite end is St. Vitus. The painter of this scene has paid more attention to living models than did those who were responsible for the Italianate work in Sta Maria Antiqua; the figures are lively and vigorous, and the quality of the work is higher than that of most of the mosaics of the same period, like those in Sta Cecilia (897-844), as well as that of most other paintings done between about 800 and 1000. There are a good many of these, for the Iconoclast ban did not extend to Italy, so that church decorations with figural subjects were not proscribed, as they were throughout so much of this age in the East.

It is not possible to discuss all the wall paintings that survive in Rome, for examples are too numerous, but a few of the most important may be mentioned, notably those in Sta Maria in Cosmedin, where there is quite an impressive figure of Christ on the triumphal arch, dating from between 858 and 867, and

---

[1] "On some Icons of the Seventh Century", in K. Weitzmann, *Late Classical and Mediaeval Studies in Honor of A. M. Friend*, Princeton, 1955.

H

those of San Bastianello on the Palatine, where the eastern apse contains an elaborate composition obviously modelled on one of the earliest Roman mosaics. In the centre of the conch is Christ with two saints on either side; below are the twelve lambs, issuing from Bethlehem and Jerusalem to approach the divine lamb, the lamb of God, in the centre. The arrangement is closely similar to that of the mosaic of Sts. Cosmas and Damian, but there are certain important features which distinguish the painting as Italian. First of these is the style itself, which is essentially Italian; second is the identity of the figures on either side of our Lord, which depict Sts. Sebastian, Lawrence, Zoticus and Stephen, who were more popular in the West than in the East; and thirdly there are certain minor details which are western, such as the bird beside our Lord's head; this is a phoenix, and Christ points at it as symbol of the Resurrection. As we have already noted, such symbolism was usual in the Catacombs, but was far less common in the Byzantine world, whereas in Italy it remained popular till quite a late date, and indeed the symbolism that constitutes so important a feature of Romanesque iconography was derived to a great extent from early Christian art in Italy.

Other examples of ninth and tenth century work could be cited, outside as well as in Rome; those at Volturno dating from between 826 and 843 may be noted, but none are very important. With the eleventh century, however, the quality improved and the quantity of examples increases, and from then on the story of the development of a new, essentially Romanesque style can be traced with but little interruption. The story may be begun once more in San Clemente, with paintings representing scenes from the lives of St. Clement and St. Alexis, done about 1100. The work is here quite westernised, both as regards style and in respect of the nature of the costumes and subsidiary details, such as tonsures, croziers, crosses, censers and so on. The decoration is rich and elaborate, the scenes very full of detail. These paintings are of real quality, though others of the period elsewhere are sometimes rather monotonous.

Once again it is impossible to cite all the churches where paintings in this new, Romanesque style are to be seen, but a few outstanding examples may be noted, and now some of the best are to be found outside, rather than in, Rome. First are those in the apse of San Pietro at Toscanella, near Viterbo;

they are in poor condition, but enough survives to show that the decoration must have been on a grand scale, though the detail is not very fine. The work was probably done under the patronage of Pope Gregory VII (1073-83). There are similar but finer paintings in the Abbey of San Pietro near Ferentillo, the most interesting of which show scenes from Genesis; the creation of Eve, and Adam naming the animals are the best known (Pl. 22, b). They show great spirit and originality, though some of the animals in the latter may derive from the old animal paradise scene, which was in turn based upon the theme of Apollo and the animals. Many of the creatures so popular in the early mosaic floors, like that of the Great Palace at Constantinople, derive from the same original sources. The paintings are to be dated to the late eleventh century.

The development of the style may be followed in the next century in the crypt of the Cathedral at Anagni, south of Rome, where there are wall paintings by three distinct hands, though all are fairly close to one another. They apparently worked under the patronage of Pope Gregory IX (1227-41). There are closely similar paintings, again essentially Romanesque, in the Sacro Speco at Subiaco, dating from 1228, and panels were done in this style as well as wall paintings; they have recently been collected in a Corpus by Mr. E. B. Garrison.[1] To-day they are preserved in a number of widely separated places, two very large and important examples being actually as far afield as in Cyprus, but many of them were probably moved after painting, and the number of workshops where these things were done must have been comparatively limited.

In addition to the Romanesque panels, quite a number of others were done in a more Byzantine style, which is usually known as the "maniera graeca". There seem to have been exponents of this style in most of the more important centres around the middle of the thirteenth century; the names of Guido da Siena working at Siena, of Coppo di Marcovaldo working at Florence, of Benedetto Berlinghieri working mainly at Lucca, and of Giunta Pisano working at Pisa, may be noted. Though Siena and Florence were soon to become the most important centres of stylistic development, Pisa and its region was a good deal more important in the earlier thirteenth century than is generally realised.

[1] *Italian Romanesque Panel Painting*, Florence, 1949.

Farther to the south developments took on a very different complexion in different regions. In Rome they were distinguished by the presence of a painter with a very personal and individual style, far closer to that of the fully developed Italian Renaissance than that of any of his contemporaries elsewhere. This man was Pietro Cavallini, and his frescoes in Sta Cecilia at Rome are works of a really outstanding character. A number of less important men seem to have worked in the same manner. South of Rome, on the eastern side of Italy, the majority of the painting that was done was far more primitive. Much of it was probably the work of monks and hermits, and it is to be found to-day in the rock-cut chapels that they used and decorated. The style is not unlike that of some of the rock-cut churches of Cappadocia in Asia Minor, and it is probable that there were links between the two areas, for the similarities are greater than could be accounted for by the fact that both lots of paintings were done for monkish patrons.

On the western side of Italy, on the other hand, work of a much more sophisticated type was being done, most of it under the patronage of the Benedictine monasteries. The main centre of development was the monastery of Monte Cassino, where Desiderius, who was abbot from 1057 till 1086, actually brought Greek craftsmen from Constantinople. What they did for him at Monte Cassino no longer survives; it had perished even before the destruction of the monastery in the campaigns of 1944 and 1945. But work which shows the influence of these Greek masters does survive elsewhere, notably in the church of St. Angelo in Formis, near Naples, which was fully decorated in the late eleventh or early twelfth century.[1] Several hands can be distinguished; some worked in an Italianate manner similar to that which dominated at Rome; others were more definitely Byzantine, and one might even have been Greek from Constantinople. Typical of this style are a winged St. Michael and a Virgin Orans supported by angels (Pl. 23). These angels are very close to Byzantine renderings both on wall and panel; a panel of the late eleventh or early twelfth century now in the Russian Museum at Leningrad is almost identical.

This Byzantine style was followed by local artists in a few

---

[1] The paintings have usually been assigned to the twelfth century, but recently Geza de Francovich has put forward a good case for assigning them to the time of Desiderius. See "Problemi della pittura e della scultura pre-Romanica", in *I Problemi comuni dell'Europa post-Carolingia*, Spoleto, 1955, pp. 475 ff.

other Benedictine houses in Italy, and from there it eventually spread to France. Wall paintings at Berzé la Ville and le Puy are typical, and in quality they perhaps surpass anything in the Benedictine style that was done on Italian soil, just as French Romanesque sculpture surpassed Italian in scope, genius and inventiveness.[1] And just as there were a number of distinct manners in the sculpture, so there were in the painting, so that the rather severe Benedictine manner which we see at Berzé la Ville was not the only style that existed. For example, a series of extremely vivid, rather more delicate, frescoes, which are in a style that is distinctly and purely French, survive at St. Savin, while others like those at Tavant on the Loire are in a more personal manner. Indeed, examples of great diversity have come to light during recent years, and their study now constitutes quite a specialised one in the story of mediaeval art. It should be undertaken alongside that of the sculptures. Space does not permit us to do more than allude to them in passing in this book, for they belong to an essentially mediaeval phase of the story of Christian art, and not to that of origins and developments, which is really the theme of our story. Nor can we do more than mention very briefly the kindred paintings of northern Spain, both on wall and panel, many of which are now preserved in the Barcelona museum. On the whole they are perhaps less important than the Romanesque paintings of France, though they constitute none the less an interesting chapter in the story of mediaeval developments.

A few further examples of wall paintings on Italian soil which are more Italian and less in the "international Benedictine style" may, however, be noted, like those in San Vicenzo at Galliano, near Como, in San Pietro di Civate, and in the Baptistry at Parma (1270). But the breath of the approaching Renaissance is much more clearly apparent in these and similar works, and they may be contrasted with some late twelfth or early thirteenth century paintings at Aquilea, where eastern elements are more prominent. The painter responsible for them was perhaps inspired by contacts with

[1] Books on French Romanesque sculpture are numerous; the most convenient one in English is that of A. Gardiner, *Mediaeval Sculpture in France*, London, 1931. But A. W. Clapham, *Romanesque Architecture in Western Europe*, Oxford, 1935, contains a useful summary, and Joan Evans, *Art in Mediaeval France, 987-1498*, Oxford, 1948, is invaluable. The story of Italian Romanesque sculpture has recently been most ably summarised by G. H. Crichton, *Italian Romanesque Sculpture*, London, 1954.

Venice, where, as we shall see, work of a completely Byzantine type was executed not only in the eleventh century, for example in the mosaics of Torcello, but also subsequently, for there was a large Greek colony there, with its own life, its own church, and where painting of a completely Byzantine type continued to be executed till as late as the seventeenth century. Indeed, el Greco, the last of the Byzantine artists, was for a time associated with this colony, and he was only following in the footsteps of numerous compatriots when he journeyed there from his native land of Crete. The difference in his case was that his art was considerably affected by western elements, whereas that of the other men remained more truly Byzantine, while again he was an individual genius of strange and outstanding ability, whereas the other men were little more than competent craftsmen. But the icons they have left for us—there is a large collection in the sacristy of San Giorgio dei Greci at Venice—are not without charm, even if they lack the transcendental glory of Greco's work.

One further monument may be noted, namely the mosaic decoration of the Baptistry at Florence. This was begun in 1225 and finished by the third decade of the next century. Though at first glance the iconography attests Byzantine relationships, and though there are Byzantine as well as Romanesque elements in the style, these mosaics are western rather than eastern. They are narrative rather than interpretational, the faces lack the intense spirituality so characteristic of Byzantine work, and many of the details are essentially western. Thus the hair dressing of the saintly figures follows a style better suited to courtesans of the day than to the holy, and the costumes of tradition and other old conventions have been discarded. The palette is also distinctive, being pale in tone, and showing little contrast. Yet in many of the scenes the role that classical models must have played is clearly apparent, and many of them would seem to have been the same models that were used by the Carolingian miniature painters and ivory carvers a few centuries earlier. St. John the Baptist's companions in the scene where he is shown communicating with them, for example, are closely similar to the personages on a Carolingian ivory at Milan.[1]

[1] For the mosaic see A. de Witt, *I Mosaici del Battistero di Firenzi*, Florence, 1955, pl. X; for the ivory see W. F Volbach, *Elfenbeinarbeiten der Spätantike und des frühen Mittelalters*, Mainz, 1952, no. 251, pl. 68.

BOOKS

E. W. ANTHONY, *Romanesque Frescoes*, Princeton, 1951.

J. HUBERT, *L'Art pré-roman*, Paris, 1938.

H. FOCILLON, *Peintures romanes des églises de France*, Paris, 1938.

CHAPTER IX

ART NORTH OF THE ALPS TILL THE TWELFTH CENTURY

WHILE the very spectacular developments discussed in the preceding chapters were taking place in Italy and, more important, in eastern Europe, the area north of the Alps had been devastated by a series of pagan barbarian invasions, and art of a non-figural character had to a great extent eclipsed that provincial Roman style that had survived for a time at least after the withdrawal of the legions. But a distinct style, figural, Christian and in the main basically classical, had developed with surprising speed as a result of the establishment of centralised control under Charlemagne, and the character of the new art was cemented by the coronation at Rome of Charlemagne as Emperor of the West in the year 800. The new art is usually known as Carolingian, and work in the same manner continued to be produced till the Carolingian dynasty gave place to the Ottonian shortly before 1000.

But though Charlemagne was crowned at Rome, and though parts of Italy were at times under his direct control and that of his successors, the court was at Aachen (Aix-la-Chapelle) in Germany, and the art and culture were essentially Germanic rather than Italian. Moreover, though we know the art of Italy best through the wall paintings, but few works on a large scale survive in the Carolingian area proper; there are virtually no sculptures, and it is the things on a small scale—illuminations, ivories and metal work—that are most characteristic of the Carolingian age as we know it. The metal, though it is sometimes rather barbaric in that it depends on a wealth of precious stones for its adornment rather than on beauty of line and detail, was often quite outstanding; the ivories boasted a very distinct iconography as well as a marked style of their own; the miniatures were probably, taken as a whole, the most important that have ever been produced by any single phase of art and culture. They are much closer to classical originals than con-

(*a*) Castelseprio. Nativity and Annunciation to the Shepherds.
Probably eighth century. (*After Weitzmann.*)

(*b*) Cappadocia. Elmale Kilisse. Christ. Twelfth century. (*Photo Powell.*)

PLATE 21

(*a*) Rome. San Clemente. Wall painting: the Ascension. 847-855.
(*Photo Anderson.*)

(*b*) Ferentillo. San Pietro. Adam naming the animals. Late eleventh century.
(*After Anthony.*)

PLATE 22

St. Angelo in Formis, near Naples. Wall painting: Archangel.
Twelfth century. (*Photo Anderson.*)

PLATE 23

(b) The Ebbo Gospels: St. Mark. 816-835. Bibliothèque
de la Ville, Epernay. (*After Boinet.*)

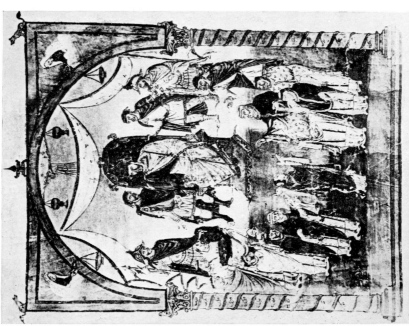

(a) Bible of Charles the Bald: title page. 844-854.
(*Photo Bibliothèque Nationale.*)

PLATE 24

temporary Byzantine work, in that old models were followed, and early themes were used rather than the more advanced Byzantine ones. At the same time the paintings were less transcendental and more straightforward—the portraits of individual emperors and patrons had a much more important part to play than was ever the case in the East or in Italy—and they were also more individual, in that a number of schools can be comparatively easily distinguished and localised, whereas in the Byzantine world this is hardly possible.

At the time that Charlemagne was crowned, the Iconoclast ban had been in force in the Byzantine world for three-quarters of a century. It was no doubt a part of Charlemagne's political policy to favour the opposite belief. In this he was supported by the Popes, who had never approved of the eastern ban on figural art. Both the Emperor and most of the Popes with him, it is true, condemned anything that actually savoured of idolatry, but it was held that even if pictures were not to be regarded as having the same importance as books for the purpose of religious edification, they still had great value. Indeed, in the western world the danger that an exaggerated reverence almost approaching idolatry might be paid to religious paintings never existed in the way that it did in the East. There, as we have seen, the feeling against even mere representation was so great that for a time art took on an entirely non-representational character. In the West the questions of representation were argued by the pedants, but they never became acute, and representation was never in danger.

Though works on a small scale were probably always outstandingly important, records of quite a number of projects for wall decorations nevertheless survive and serve to attest that work on a large scale was indeed done all over the Carolingian world. Thus at Ingelheim the whole church was painted under the patronage of Louis the Pious; Old Testament scenes were on the left and New Testament scenes on the right, presumably balancing one another with regard to subject, in the way that was much favoured from the sixth century onwards (see p. 75). A similar decoration was set up in the monastery church at St. Gall, and there were no doubt others elsewhere. None of these survives, but recently an elaborate decoration of the early ninth century has been discovered in the minster at Müstair in

Switzerland,[1] which again comprises a full series of Old and New Testament scenes. Like much Carolingian art, the work is already distinctively western both in style and iconography, though certain eastern, more particularly Syrian, elements are present. As in the case of the wall paintings in south Italy, this influence seems to have penetrated direct without touching Constantinople; but that links with the hub of the Byzantine world also existed is suggested by the nature of another decoration, this time in mosaic, which was set up by Theodolphus, Bishop of Orleans between 805 and 811, in a small church at St. Germigny des Pres. These mosaics are a great deal more Byzantine in character. The church is of the apsed cross-in-square plan, and is distinctly eastern in type; the mosaics, which show winged angels very like those in St. Angelo in Formis, now survive only in the eastern apse; originally there were probably other mosaics in the other apses also.

Though the revival of classical elements was the most essential feature of Carolingian art, and though such eastern elements as appear were often due to contacts with Syria, Constantinopolitan influence also played a part in the growth of the Carolingian style. There were frequent interchanges of ideas, Byzantine objects were imported and copied, and the numerous ambassadors who came from the Emperor at Constantinople to the West brought with them presents of silks and ivory, which were treasured and imitated. Direct copying of Byzantine models took place from time to time, but it must not be forgotten that some of the resemblances that are to be observed to-day between Carolingian and Byzantine works are due to the fact that both Carolingian and Byzantine art owed a debt to the same Early Christian prototypes, and in the field of manuscript illumination, where the copyists tended to reproduce the old illustrations faithfully and exactly, in the same way that they reproduced the texts, the continued survival of old ideas in both areas was assured. For this very reason the manuscript illustrations tend on the whole to be more conservative than other forms of art, except where the other works show the inspiration of the manuscripts, as do many of the ivories. Such works as the Bible of Count Vivien[2] and the Gospels of

---

[1] L. Birchler, "Zur Karolingischen Architektur und Malerei in Münster-Müstair", in *Frühmittelalterliche Kunst*, Lausanne, 1954.

[2] Morey, *Art Bulletin*, VII, 1924, fig. 39.

Charlemagne are thus in a distinctly classical style, though they were produced in the ninth century. Their illustrations are not unlike those of certain of the more retrospective works that were done at Constantinople, not so much because of any inter-connection but because both made use of the same early Christian or late classical models. The same is true of many of the Carolingian ivories; often it would be far from easy to tell them from East Christian ones,[1] were it not for certain icono-graphical details culled from the classical world which were preserved in the West, though they were replaced by other themes in the East. The most important is the youthful, beard-less Christ, which was well nigh as universal in the West after the eighth century as the bearded variant was typical of the East. Similarly, in the scene of the Entry into Jerusalem Christ usually sits astride the donkey in the West, whereas in the East He rides sideways in accordance with local practice.

The similarities that many of the surviving manuscript illustrations and ivories show to one another suggest that quite a number of early manuscripts which have now disappeared must have been in existence early in the Carolingian era, for it is only if we accept that they were available as models that the similarities can be accounted for. Thus a Bible in the British Museum (the Moutier-Grandval Bible), done between 834 and 843, and the Bible of Charles the Bald in the Bibliothèque Nationale, done between 844 and 854 (Pl. 24, a), are closely akin and obviously follow the same prototype, though the prototype has not survived. The Bible of Charles the Fat in St. Paul's-outside-the-walls at Rome, done around 880, was clearly modelled on the Ashburnham Pentateuch, one of the few western manuscripts of pre-Carolingian date that survive, while the famous Utrecht Psalter, done at Rheims about 800, also follows an earlier prototype, which must have been closely similar in style to the Joshua Roll.

Very soon after the foundation of the Carolingian empire, if not indeed before, a great activity in copying manuscripts began to take place, and even before the middle of the ninth century a number of different schools were in being. Thanks to the penetrating researches of a number of scholars, most of these schools can now be clearly distinguished. Goldschmidt thus

---

[1] See for example the plates in W. F. Volbach, *Elfenbeinarbeiten der Spätantike und des frühen Mittelalters*, Mainz, 1952.

notes what are known as the Ada, the Liuthard and the Metz groups. The first of these was associated with the capital at Aachen and was characterised by a rather hard monumental manner; work of the Liuthard group was more delicate and refined; the work of the Metz school, being associated with a place rather than an individual, was more diverse. To these stylistic groups may be added a number of local schools, notably those of Tours, Corbie and Rheims. In all of these places work of an individual character was done. The nervous, linear style of Rheims was particularly individual. Its character is illustrated at its best by the line drawings of the Utrecht Psalter (Pl. 27, *a*), but in some of the Rheims work the line was so nervous that it might almost be called jittery; the portraits of the Evangelists in the Ebbo Gospels, now at Epernay, serve to illustrate this extreme manner (Pl. 24, *b*).

The problem of distinguishing the schools in greater detail is one of specialised scholarship rather than of general art history, and is hardly possible without a mass of illustrations. It has progressed very considerably in recent years and it is now possible to be sure of the characteristics of all the major schools and to associate with one or another of them practically every manuscript that has come down to us. Such localisation is quite impossible in the Byzantine world, where, even if groups can be distinguished on stylistic grounds, it is still extremely difficult to associate them even with widely separated regions, let alone with towns or particular workshops. It would thus seem that the style and taste of the individual artist had a far greater role to play in the West than in the East, and this is borne out by another factor characteristic of all these schools, namely the attention paid to portraiture. There is hardly a manuscript that does not contain at least one portrait. They vary from single figures showing the patron for whom the book was done to ceremonial groups. Most of the personages have clearly been done from the life; they show both personality and individuality, and are often very striking pictures. They contrast markedly with the Evangelist portraits, at the commencements of the Gospels, which are much more conventional, and follow older models, often the same models as those used by Byzantine illuminators. The Evangelists are also in most cases shown against landscape or architectural backgrounds—both must ultimately have been derived from Pompeian models—whereas the Carolingian Emperors are usually enthroned, and are surrounded by a number of subsidiary figures in addition to the main one but on a reduced scale. There is, too, more often than not, a mass of minor details in each picture. Such realistic portraits were hardly attempted in the Byzantine world, where imperial panoply always took precedence over individuality.

In addition to the imperial portraits and the usual Bible scenes, decorative architectural compositions were also in great favour. These were generally based on the classical tholos, which was often developed into a sort of three-storeyed pagoda of great charm and fantasy; the most effective is probably that in the Gospels of St. Médard of Soissons, where it is to be interpreted as a portrayal of the fountain of life (Pl. 25, a). Never were such fantasies attempted in Byzantine manuscripts, though the frames of the calendar tables were sometimes quite elaborate. But the Damascus mosaics are comparable in theme and fantasy. Both must have been ultimately derived from the same antique models.

The majority of the surviving Carolingian manuscripts are grand and impressive, and reflect very clearly the nature of the society for which they were produced, an imperial one, where mundane glory, even in ecclesiastical circles, was of great significance. A similar picture is presented by the metal work, which in the main consists of imperial regalia—crowns, swords, spears and so forth. True, many of these things were of a symbolical character, and had a sacred role to play, and some were even believed to be made from such relics as the nails of the true cross. But their very character distinguishes them just as much as their style from the treasures of the Byzantine world, which most often took the form of chalices, patens or gospel covers. In the one area ecclesiastic form permeated every facet of life; in the other the panoply of a worldly, battle-loving emperor was hallowed in the service of the faith. We see here the very features which distinguish western from eastern Christianity to the present time. In the East the spiritual world exists and flourishes in its own right, and is something distinct from the world of every day. In the West mundane forms dominate even in spiritual affairs, and the two are closely knit together. It is thus not surprising that the majority of the manuscripts are grand and impressive, rather than esoteric or transcendental.

One manuscript, however, may be selected for special mention, namely the Utrecht Psalter (Pl. 27, *a*). It is of a very different type. It was done at Rheims soon after 800, and its illustrations consist of a series of line drawings depicting passages of the Psalms and interpolated at intervals in the text. The figures are disposed against landscape backgrounds. The drawing is very delicate and refined, the figures extremely expressive. They illustrate the Psalms with which they are associated most vividly, though the themes are at first glance sometimes rather confusing, in that they show what are clearly New Testament subjects; such scenes were put in when the Psalms foretell events which were subsequently enacted in our Lord's life. For example, the words of Psalm XVI, "Neither wilt thou suffer thine Holy One to see corruption", are illustrated by the well-known scene of the Resurrection, rendered as the Three Marys at the Sepulchre.

Not only is this manuscript a very lovely thing in itself, but it has a special significance for the history of English art, for it found its way to Canterbury at quite an early date and remained there for some centuries. It was copied there on several occasions, its style was deeply assimilated, and it is to a great extent owing to its influence that a mass of very distinctive and very lovely manuscripts were produced at Canterbury and elsewhere in England in the tenth and early eleventh centuries, the majority of them in the same linear manner. The marriage of the expressive, nervous style of the Utrecht Psalter with the decorative heritage of the Hiberno-Saxon school was probably the main influence behind the development of later Saxon painting.

The tradition not only of the Utrecht Psalter but also of many of the other manuscripts of Carolingian times, was even more influential on the Continent, and the next phase of culture there, the Ottonian, was in the main a revival and development of the old Carolingian, though classical influence was progressively subordinated, on the one hand as a result of intensified contacts with the Byzantine world, and on the other owing to the spontaneous growth of a new, more abstract approach on the part of the artists themselves.

The new dynasty came into power in 919, but it was the second king of the line, Otto I, who gave it his name, and his coronation at Aachen, Charlemagne's old capital, served as a tangible indication of his aim to found an empire greater than the old Saxon kingdom which his father Henry I had ruled. A second coronation by the Pope at Rome in 962 marked the accomplishment of his aims, even though no more than a small part of Italy was ever subject to his rule. Considerable tracts of the country still remained under direct Byzantine control, and Byzantine artistic influence was rife over the whole land; it was in this way that the renewal of Byzantine influence in the Ottonian world was brought about, though the casual contacts were cemented on the one hand by exchanges of embassies, and on the other by the marriage of Otto I's son and successor to the Byzantine princess Theophano. An ivory showing the coronation of this queen and her consort, Otto II, by Christ, which is now in the Cluny Museum in Paris, serves as tangible proof of this Byzantine influence, for it made use of an established Byzantine theme now represented by two ivories of similar crownings which are preserved in the Bibliothèque Nationale in Paris and in the Historical Museum at Moscow.[1]

Though many of the ivories and miniatures indicate a new interest in the depiction of biblical scenes, and though they concentrate more on pure narrative than was usual in Carolingian works, it was in the development of a new, more abstract, more expressive type of art that the Ottonian age was perhaps most distinguished. True, a few manuscripts, like the Codex Egberti, were fairly close to Carolingian ones, though a tendency to eliminate the architectural or landscape backgrounds became apparent at an early date, as well as one towards the stylisation of subsidiary details, like trees, which are, in most of the Ottonian manuscripts, rather like oversize mushroom plants. But, in general, progress towards abstraction was carried a good deal farther, even when backgrounds were present. The figures were thus usually poised in space, no effort being made to plant them on the ground in a secure manner; they became strangely elongated and emaciated, with immense hands and great staring eyes, and though the nature of the story they tell is still clear enough, its expression at times became almost grotesque; the Washing of Feet in the Gospels

---

[1] The former shows the coronation of Romanos and Eudoxia; it is probably Romanos II (959) rather than Romanos IV (1068); see *Byzantine Art*, pl. 52. The latter shows that of Constantine VII Porphyrogenitus (913).

of Otto III (985-1002), the Entry into Jerusalem in the "Peri-kop book" of Henry II or the portrait of the Evangelist John in the Amiens Gospels may be cited as examples (Pl. 25, *b*). Were it not so obviously sincere, much of this art would arouse attention only because of its curiosity. It sought no doubt the same transcendental ends as did Byzantine art, but the abstractions and in many cases the obvious incompetence of the artists reduced much of it to the standard of "primitive" rather than "fine" art, even though patronage was lavish and the materials, such as gold leaf, were rare and costly.

The illumination of manuscripts apparently continued at all the centres where schools had existed in Carolingian times, namely Aachen, Metz, Rheims, Tours and Corbie, but to these centres were added others, such as Reichenau, Goldbach, Hildesheim and Ratisbon, and activity was very considerable, in any case till after the year 1050. Whether much work was done in the way of wall painting is uncertain, for little has survived, but it is probable that it was, for it is to this age that we owe the revival of metal working on a large scale under the patronage of Bishop Bernward of Hildesheim (1008-52). To the numerous book covers, crosses and similar small-scale works may thus be added the curious column with relief decoration up its surface in a spiral, as on Trajan's column at Rome, and the very impressive bronze doors at Hildesheim which were done to the Bishop's order. The figures on the doors are in quite high relief, and though they have the same strangely emaciated character as those in the miniatures, they show at the same time a new interest in anatomy for its own sake. In fact, they herald the new age and style, which saw its final culmination in early Gothic art. The same is true of a number of other sculptures on a large scale done in Germany around the middle of the eleventh century, most of them Crucifixions. Examples in bronze, like that at Werden, and in wood, are comparatively numerous.[1]

If these large sculptures herald a new age, those on a smaller scale were in the main more conservative, and it is here not always very easy to distinguish the Ottonian from the Carol-ingian products. A number of crowns, state swords and similar pieces of imperial regalia of Carolingian character thus survive, but the book covers, richly adorned with precious

[1] For plates of these see C. R. Morey, *Mediaeval Art*, figs. 73 ff.

(b) The Amiens Gospels: St. John. Tenth century.

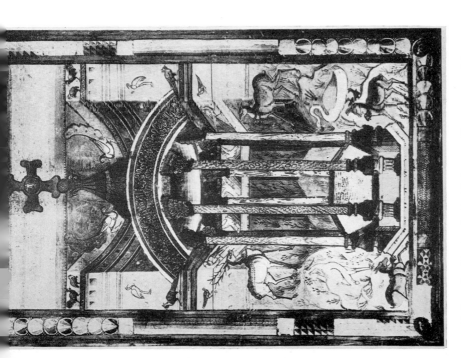

(a) Gospels of St. Médard of Soissons. First quarter of the ninth century. (*Photo Bibliothèque Nationale.*)

PLATE 25

(b) Page from the Book of Kells: the Temptation of Christ. c. 800. Trinity College, Dublin. (Photo Baldwin Brown.)

(a) The Book of Lindisfarne: St. Matthew. Late seventh century. British Museum. (Photo Baldwin Brown.)

stones, and reliquaries, some of them of very great elaboration, are probably more characteristic. They were produced in numerous centres in addition to Hildesheim. There were also several places where enamel work was done; the most important of them was Regensburg. The enamels often followed Byzantine models closely.

During the later tenth and earlier eleventh centuries, developments in France were far behind those in Germany. It may be that the old belief that the world would end in the year 1000 exercised greater sway there; it may be that the capital and court were too far away. But whatever the reason, it was not until the mid eleventh century that things began to move in France with any very considerable momentum. But when movement finally started, it was very rapid, and from about 1050 onwards artistic developments were quite astonishing. From the almost childish efforts of the middle of the century, stone sculpture had achieved, by around 1100, some of the greatest glories ever accomplished in carving; the capitals of the choir at Cluny or the portals of Autun, Moissac or Vezelay may be noted as examples. From the small, unambitious, rather crude "basilicas" of the first Romanesque style the architects had developed a manner of church building which was by 1100 one of the world's truly great architectural styles. The great third church at Cluny, finished just before 1100, should be considered, along with Justinian's Sancta Sophia and St. Peter's at Rome, as one of the world's three greatest Christian buildings.

No truly comparable strides were made in Germany; with the decline of the Ottonian dynasty, the scene of progress moved to France and a new patronage, that of Benedictine monasticism, replaced that of the Imperial house. With it a new age dawned, which is outside the story of the earlier phases of Christian art. It was an age of astonishing progress and of great accomplishment, and though the name of the new style "Romanesque" suggests a derivation from Rome, the implication presents a false picture. There is but little that is Roman about the style; it is its newness that is its distinction, and it is as the manifestation of an intrinsically new art that Romanesque should be studied.

I

BOOKS

A. BOINET, *La Miniature carolingienne*, Paris, 1913 (plates only).

R. HINKS, *Carolingian Art*, London, 1935.

H. JANTZEN, *Ottonische Kunst*, Munich, 1949.

CHAPTER X

EARLY CHRISTIAN ART IN BRITAIN

ONE of the most remarkable factors in connection with the story of early Christian art is that work of really outstanding quality was produced in the British Isles at a date well in advance of anything on the Continent north of the Alps. Thus, though little that was not basically barbarous was done in France or Germany before the coronation of Charlemagne in 800, in Northumbria sculpture, metal work and illumination that was both outstandingly fine and also essentially sophisticated was done at least a century and a quarter earlier. An art that was already basically Christian probably came to this country from the Mediterranean world along with the first missions, that of Columba to Scotland in 563 and that of St. Augustine to southern England in 597. Nothing is, however, known from these early times, though it may well be that artists who had been schooled in the Byzantine tradition came from Italy in the seventh century in search of adventure or employment, or even perhaps as refugees, driven from their homeland by Gothic invasions or as a result of the unstable conditions which followed upon the break-up of Justinian's empire. All that we do know is that the first dated monuments were not only very Byzantine in style but also of extremely high quality.

The most important of these early works are to be found in Northumbria, though there was another advanced school in existence at much the same time in the south. In both areas alike the story begins in the last quarter of the seventh century, after the disputes between the two rival sects of the faith, the Celtic in the north and the Roman in the south, had been ended as a result of the Council of Whitby in 664. Church building and decoration flourished, and the records tell of a great activity. Not a few buildings of this age actually survive; the two most important are probably the church at Brixworth (c. 670) and that at Escomb (late seventh century). All were on a small scale, of rough masonry, though well built, and usually

FIG. 12.   Carving on St. Cuthbert's coffin.   Late seventh century.
The Cathedral library, Durham.

of considerable height in comparison to the area. Whether or not they were decorated with sculptures is uncertain, for no pieces of architectural sculpture survive; the earliest carvings that we have are simple, crude crosses carved on grave slabs, and the first hints of elaboration appear on another sepulchral monument, the wooden coffin of St. Cuthbert at Durham (Fig. 12). It bears figural work of a rather primitive character which is really little more than rough line engraving. The date of these carvings has been disputed, though one in the last quarter of the seventh century seems most likely. It is rather surprising that these carvings should be so crude, for on the one hand St. Cuthbert was a figure of great importance and sanctity, and one would have expected to see the finest work associated with his coffin, while on the other at almost exactly the same date stone carvers were producing sculptures of far finer quality near by.

This fine work appears not on stones intended to be used inside buildings but on the great stone crosses which were set up over graves or sometimes perhaps on sites which had been sacred in pagan times, and which it was desired to hallow in the service of the new faith. The crosses, in fact, took the place and also took on the role of the old pagan menhirs or standing stones. There were once considerable numbers of these crosses, but two, those at Bewcastle and Ruthwell, close to the Scottish border, are especially striking. They are of considerable size, and the work is of very high quality, especially if allowance is made for the fact that the surviving examples have stood in the open air of a northern climate, swept by wind and exposed to rain, snow and frost, for some twelve hundred years.

The figural work on these crosses must have been considerably influenced from the Mediterranean world, both with regard to style and iconography. Perhaps actual artisans from the East reached Britain; perhaps imported models, in the form of ivories, were used. Indeed, the fact that the scene of Christ treading on the asp and basilisk is shown in almost exactly the same way on the Bewcastle cross as on the Ruthwell one makes the latter supposition the more probable (Fig. 13). The elaborate vine and ivy scrolls which appear again suggest the use of an imported model; those on the Ruthwell cross, for example, are closely similar to some on the ivories of the throne of Maximian at Ravenna.

FIG. 13. Christ treading on the Asp and Basilisk.
The Bewcastle cross. Late seventh century.

But not all the ornament was naturalistic. Much of it belongs in fact to a quite different family, where stress was laid not on naturalism and representation but on formalism and pattern. The Bewcastle cross itself bears ornament of this type (Fig. 14),

FIG. 14. Interlacing ornament on the Bewcastle cross.
Late seventh century.

and it became more and more important in the carvings of the later eighth and early ninth centuries. The sources of this art are to be found in the northern world, and it was to a great extent thanks to links with Scandinavia that the style was developed in Britain, even if, ultimately, this formal, non-representational art had its origins in the middle East.

Though much of this early sculpture was of very high quality—the Ruthwell and Bewcastle crosses are by no means the only examples—the most characteristically British art was perhaps not sculpture but illumination. Here the abstract, non-representational style was given a completely free rein, and a great deal of exquisite work was done, both in the way of full-page illuminations and in that of single letters at the beginnings of chapters or paragraphs. Quite a number of manuscripts survive, and a good deal of dispute has raged as to their respective dates and as to where this art of illumination was first developed, one school of thought claiming the honour for Ireland and another for Northumbria. Actually there are two fairly distinct styles, a more linear one, where human figures play a part, if only a minor one, and a more wholly decorative. The Book of Lindisfarne is characteristic of the first of these styles, the Book of Durrow of the second. But they are obviously very closely related, and the differences are no more than those one would expect to find between different workshops of the same school. It is possible that the style of Lindisfarne is characterised by the former book and that of some place in Ireland by the latter. No doubt such work was also done in the island of Iona, where St. Columba landed and founded what was to become the most important monastery in the north of Britain at the time these books were done.

The Book of Durrow, now at Trinity College, Dublin, is probably the earliest of these manuscripts that survive, and is to be dated to the last quarter of the seventh century. It contains virtually no figural work, for such figures as are present are completely un-naturalistic, and much of the formal ornament is close to that which we see on pre-Christian objects such as the famous hanging bowls. The drawing is on the whole thick and heavy, and lacks something of the ease and flow of that in the Lindisfarne Gospels. It is, in fact, a conservative work, still not far removed from the style usual on metal work in pagan times. The Book of Lindisfarne, on the other hand, is more advanced and shows evidence of closer contacts with the Mediterranean world. It was probably done on the island of the same name shortly before the year 700. Here the pattern work is extremely elaborate and varied. Old Celtic motifs of pagan type are still present, but the rendering shows a new approach, and it is the brilliant freshness of the work that distinguishes the book above all else. In addition to the pattern work, there are four portraits of Evangelists. These follow early Christian prototypes fairly closely, though much of the detail that must have been present in the models, such as arcades, thrones and so on, is absent. A particularly interesting feature is that the name of each Evangelist is preceded by the Greek word for saint, agios, instead of the Latin, sanctus, though written in Latin script (Pl. 26, a). The use of the Greek word suggests that a Byzantine model was used, even if at second rather than first remove.

The figures in the Lindisfarne manuscript are perhaps not very proficient, but they show nevertheless some understanding of the figural models. Where figures occur in the Book of Kells they show no such understanding. The Madonna is gaunt and ugly, the Child on her knee grotesque, and such scenes as appear, like the temptation of Christ on the pinnacle of the temple by the Devil, are almost unrecognisable (Pl. 26, *b*). But the pattern work reaches a degree of excellence never previously achieved and never afterwards surpassed. It is a sheer delight, and the illuminations of this book are to be counted as works of art of a very high standard, even if they do not follow nature or tell any very clear story. The book is to be dated to around the year 800, but it is not easy to say exactly where it was done. The monastery of Kells in Ireland, the name of which it bears, is as likely to be the home as anywhere else. The monastery on Iona is also possible.

In the south of Britain links with early Christian art and the Mediterranean world were far closer, though the results were less successful from the artistic point of view. The Codex Aureus, now at Stockholm, but probably done at Canterbury in the later eighth century, is of this type. It contains the usual Evangelist portraits, representing them seated frontally in niches, with curtains looped up on either side, just like those on some of the mosaics of S. Apollinare Nuovo at Ravenna. But the figures are wooden, the surroundings heavy and clumsy, and all the charm and fantasy of the Northumbrian books is lacking; even the portraits in the Book of Lindisfarne seem more inspired. The southern manuscripts, indeed, bear out the testimony of the other arts, especially sculpture and metal work, namely that the south of England was far less advanced than the north at this time. At a later date culture, thought and art were to be developed there to a very marked degree, and a new style of illumination came into being under the influence of new contacts with the Continent and the Mediterranean. But until the Renaissance of Alfred, the north, and subsequently Mercia in the centre, were the centres of greatest and most advanced activity.

The northern style of illumination in the eighth century was not restricted to Britain, and there seems to have been a good deal of give and take with monasteries on the Continent. Works of art as well as monks found their way overseas, and quite a lot of illumination was done in such Continental monasteries as Bobbio and St. Gall in the Northumbrian or Irish manner. Hints of the style indeed continued to crop up in Continental

FIG. 15. Sculptured cross, Codford St. Peter.
Late ninth century.

work for a century or so, though the formal pattern motifs that were so characteristic gradually became subordinated to those of a more naturalistic type.

After these very brilliant beginnings the quality of art in Britain somewhat declined, primarily as a result of Norse raids and lootings, and as the eighth century progressed, the power of Northumbria gradually waned. With the next century the main centre of culture had moved southwards, to Mercia; a century later again it was established in the full south, in Wessex, and only then were the full glories restored. But some work of interest, especially in the sphere of sculpture, was done in Mercia in the ninth century; the most important surviving examples are some friezes with acanthus scrolls and some slabs with figures upon them at Breedon in Leicestershire. Once more these show Continental, ultimately Byzantine, influence.

It was, however, only with the revival of culture under Alfred and his successors that art of real quality once more began to be produced. Its style was new and quite distinct, more sophisticated than in earlier times, and also very much more English. Indeed, it was perhaps the essential Englishness of this art that constituted its most outstanding characteristic. The best work was produced from about the middle of the tenth century onwards, until a new style replaced it as a result of the Norman conquest. It showed remarkable accomplishment even in small, out-of-the-way places, while work done under the influence of what may best be termed the court school was invariably quite outstanding.

The new manner of later Saxon art appears for the first time in an embryo stage in an extremely original, but at the same time very lovely, tall stone at Codford St. Peter in Wiltshire, which is probably to be dated to the end of the ninth century (Fig. 15). It cannot be said that there is much Byzantine influence present here; the style is, rather, completely and essentially English, and heralds that of a great deal of work done in the second half of the tenth century, more especially in the illuminations of the so called Winchester school. Before saying something about this school, however, a few more pieces of sculpture may be noted, for it would seem that in its own way stone sculpture was just as important in Wessex in late Saxon times as it had been in Northumbria in the seventh and early eighth centuries. Two of the most interesting pieces of

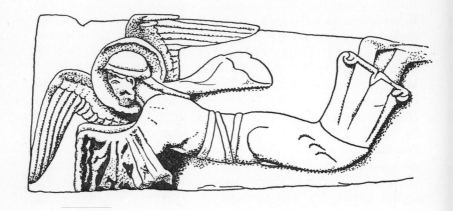

FIG. 16. Stone sculpture, two angels. Bradford on Avon.
Tenth century.

work, done perhaps before or soon after the middle of the tenth century, are matching sculptures showing two angels confronted, at Bradford on Avon (Fig. 16). They probably stood on either side of a Crucifixion scene. These are much more Byzantine than the Codford St. Peter stone, and it is possible that an imported ivory was used as a model. The same is true of a very lovely rendering of the Crucified Christ at Romsey in Hampshire (Fig. 17). Its iconography is completely conventional, unlike that of the Codford sculpture. But another great Crucifixion, at Langford in Oxfordshire, may be contrasted (Fig. 18), for here the Christ wears a long monkish robe, bound by a cord at the waist. This follows an entirely distinct iconographical tradition, derived perhaps originally from Syria, but developed later in Germany and elsewhere on the Continent, in regions independent of the Byzantine world. There are other sculptures in quite a number of village churches of the south, most of them in an essentially English style akin to that of the miniatures.

The same styles and the same trends that characterised the development of stone sculpture are to be seen in the ivories. Some are thus completely English, like a plaque in the Victoria and Albert Museum bearing the Adoration of the Magi and another akin to it, but rather less sophisticated, in the Louvre, representing the Virgin and Child.[1] Others are akin to work done on the Continent, showing either the influence of the earlier Carolingian art or that of what was being done at much the same time under the Ottonian emperors in southern Germany. A very lovely Crucifixion in the Victoria and Albert Museum, set on a metal mount of German workmanship, is more closely related to the Continent, though it is certainly an English work. The head of a T-shaped cross in the British Museum, known as the Alcester Tau, is on the other hand more English, both as regards its workmanship and in the actual form, for these T-shaped crosses were more usual in this country than overseas. What is probably the finest of all the ivories, a crozier head in the Victoria and Albert Museum, is again essentially English, and some of the figures suggest relationships with paintings of the "Winchester" school. Its date has been disputed, some thinking that it should be assigned to the early eleventh century, and some that it could only have been

[1] For these and other ivories see M. H. Longhurst, *English Ivories*, London, 1926.

FIG. 17. The Romsey Rood, Hampshire.
Early eleventh century.

Fig. 18. The Langford Rood, Oxfordshire.
Late tenth or early eleventh century.

done after the Conquest. Whenever it was carved, however, elements of the true late Saxon style are undoubtedly present.

The miniatures of later Saxon times are, on the whole, probably more generally familiar than the stone sculptures and ivory carvings. Happily quite a considerable number of examples survive, and they extend in date from those done early in the tenth century, where not very inspiring interlacing patterns derived from Northumbrian art are to the fore, to manuscripts illustrated in the later tenth and the first half of the eleventh centuries, with scenes from the Bible story, told at length in full-page illuminations. These scenes were invariably enclosed in elaborate borders of rosettes, acanthus leaves and sometimes even a sort of trellis work, which are often very lovely in themselves. They constitute what is virtually a hall-mark of the Anglo-Saxon style.

The manuscripts can be divided into two groups, those in which the illustrations are in line only and those where they are elaborately coloured. The colouring itself is often of great beauty, though it is usually decorative rather than naturalistic, in that the men have blue hair and so on. But the drawing, whether alone or as a basis for the coloured work, shows that close attention was paid to nature; there is usually an astonishing vividness and power of expression. Work was done in a number of different centres, of which Winchester and Canterbury were probably the most important. Illustrations in line and in colour seem to have been done equally in all of them. At first the more important schools were in the south, and such places as Bury St. Edmunds in the east and Hereford in the West Country boasted flourishing schools of illumination. Later production spread to the north also, and it is likely that good work was done at York, and certain that manuscripts were illustrated at Durham.

Of the manuscripts with illustrations in line, a copy of the Utrecht Psalter, which was made at Canterbury about 1000, is perhaps the finest; it is now in the British Museum, and it is interesting to compare the copy with the original (Pl. 27). The copyist sometimes misjudged the space available, so that his figures do not always fit in as they should, but his line is perhaps more tender and delicate. A manuscript now in the Bodleian at Oxford, known as the Caedmon manuscript, is similar in style and is in some ways more interesting, for its illustrations are

(a) The Utrecht Psalter. c. 800. (After de Wald.)

(b) Page from the Canterbury Manuscript (Harley 603). c. 1000.
(Photo British Museum.)

Illustrations to Psalm 104

PLATE 27

The Benedictional of St. Æthelwold: the Marys at the Sepulchre. 975-980.
Chatsworth. (*Photo Courtauld Institute.*)

PLATE 28

new and original, and include a number of scenes which do not appear to have been illustrated previously. The draftsman thus had to create, not merely to copy with understanding, as was the case with the man who did the copy of the Utrecht Psalter.

Of the manuscripts with coloured illustrations, the most elaborate is probably the Benedictional of St. Æthelwold at Chatsworth, which was done at Winchester between 975 and 980. It contains a large number of Bible scenes, all framed in the characteristic rosette borders (Pl. 28). There are other similar but rather less elaborate manuscripts in a number of libraries in this country, and others are to be found on the Continent, where they were mostly taken soon after the Norman conquest. The most important of these are two manuscripts at Rouen, known as the Benedictional of Archbishop Robert (c. 980) and the Sacramentary of Robert of Jumièges (c. 1008). All are fine and serve to show the individuality as well as the distinction and quality of English art at this time.

In addition to the full-page illustrations representing Bible scenes, many of the manuscripts also contain a number of fine initials, done with the same richness of foliage as the rosette borders. These are not only lovely in themselves, but are also important in respect of the long heritage that they left behind them. Though new motifs and new styles were introduced almost immediately as a result of the Norman conquest, the old foliage ornament was interpolated, and its style survived in English work almost until Gothic times.

In addition to the arts we have considered so far—sculptures in stone, ivories and illuminations—work of quality appears to have been done in practically every field of art. We know nothing of wall paintings, though they probably existed; the fragments of pottery that have been found suggest that fine work was done, some of it of a rather Byzantine type; metal work and jewellery were outstanding; most important of all, superb textiles were produced. Of the works in metal, the most important is a gold jewel shaped like a pear, with a cloisonné enamel on one side, now in the Ashmolean Museum at Oxford, which is known as the Alfred jewel. An inscription on the side states that it was made for Alfred, and it must date from the last quarter of the ninth century. Of the textiles, the most famous is a narrow embroidered band now at Durham known as the stole of St. Cuthbert. It was made between 909 and 916, and

K

was presumably introduced into his tomb about the same time. It bears portraits of the prophets, with their names beside them in Latin script; the iconography and the style are basically Byzantine, and it would seem likely that the women who embroidered the figures worked from a Byzantine model, perhaps an illumination. Though not many other pieces of embroidery survive, there are frequent references to the importance of English work at this time, and indeed it was famed, under the name of "opus Anglicanum", all over the civilised world.

Though it belongs to the next phase of culture, the fully fledged mediaeval rather than the early Christian, one other piece of embroidery may be noted, for its style shows clearly the influence of the Saxon illuminations and line drawings. It is the remarkable textile now at Bayeux, known as the Bayeux Tapestry, and it was probably done in this country soon after the Norman conquest. It tells the story of Harold's visit to Normandy, of the death of King Edward the Confessor, of Harold's assumption of royal power, and of the consequent invasion of England by William with extraordinary vividness, and in the main with astonishing impartiality. The tale is told, and it is left to the beholder to take sides as he wishes. It is a fine and very important work, though because of its secular character it hardly concerns us in this book. But it serves as a fitting tribute to the power and quality of English art at this time, when an old age was ending and a new one dawning.

BOOKS

A. W. Clapham, *English Romanesque Architecture before the Conquest*, Oxford, 1930.

T. D. Kendrick, *Saxon Art to 900*, London, 1938, and *Late Saxon and Viking Art*, London, 1949.

D. Talbot Rice, *English Art, 871-1100*, Oxford, 1952.

Part IV

THE SECOND FLOWERING IN THE EAST

In the year 726 an edict forbidding the representation of saintly or divine form in art was passed at Constantinople, and except for a brief interlude, it remained in force until 843. In out-of-the-way regions it was probably never very strictly enforced, but in the capital and the larger cities mosaics were torn down in the churches and paintings destroyed; its enforcement is indeed one of the reasons why so little is preserved from early times in the East. With the return to an official recognition of figural art in 843, however, there dawned an age of exceptional brilliance. It is usually known as the "Second Golden Age" of Byzantine art. It was distinguished by great architectural activity, by the erection of numerous rich decorations in mosaic, by great developments of wall painting as a decoration for church interiors, and by the production of an immense wealth of objects on a small scale, in metal, ivory, precious stones or textiles. The great wealth and high quality of these minor arts have indeed earned for Byzantine art of this age the appellation "sumptuous". But these smaller things were not only rich but also of great artistic quality. In many ways they represent Byzantine art in its most characteristic form. At one time it was held that Byzantine art of this "Second Golden Age" showed little variation between 843 and the year 1204, when the Fourth Crusade sacked Constantinople. But more detailed research has disclosed that this was not so; new ideas were introduced and styles changed from age to age; especially important was the development of a new, profoundly humanistic outlook in the twelfth century, which led to what is best called the Byzantine Revival.

CHAPTER XI

BYZANTINE ART IN THE NINTH, TENTH AND ELEVENTH CENTURIES

IF the Joshua Roll, the Paris Psalter and the Castelseprio frescoes should indeed be dated after Iconoclasm, as Weitzmann suggests, the assumption is that they should be associated with the conscious classical revival brought about by Constantine Porphyrogenitus (913-959). Iconoclasm, however, ended finally in 843, so that more than half a century elapsed before this classical revival began. What happened in the interval? Happily a few major works survive in the East that can definitely be assigned to this age. Most important from the historical point of view are some very fragmentary mosaics in a chamber above the south porch in Sancta Sophia at Constantinople, which must have been put up immediately after the lifting of the Iconoclast ban. Some mosaics at Nicaea and others in Sancta Sophia at Salonica are of much the same date and are more interesting artistically.

The Constantinopolitan mosaics are important because they include a portrait of Methodius, the Patriarch who presided over the council which sanctioned the return to images[1]; they must have been set up during his lifetime. The mosaics at Nicaea no longer survive, but there are good photographs, and these and studies made on the spot before their destruction about 1920 suggest that the Virgin in the apse must be dated either to about 850, or to the age of Irene, when the ban was temporarily lifted, that is to between 797 and 802. Indeed, the historical evidence favours this earlier date, though one wonders how mosaics escaped destruction at a place so near the capital when once the ban was reinforced. The detail of the work is excellent and the tall full-length figure of the Virgin is extremely impressive (Pl. 20, *b*). It is one of the few surviving examples of a type which was certainly very important from

[1] P. A. Underwood, "A preliminary report on some unpublished mosaics in Hagia Sophia", *American Journal of Archaeology*, 55, 1951, p. 367.

that time onwards. Other examples are of much later date, notably those in the apses at Torcello and Murano. The same iconography was frequently followed on a smaller scale, as for example in a lovely ivory now at Utrecht, which must date from the late eleventh century (Pl. 30, *a*). Though the disposition of the figures altered little as time went on, the conception changed, becoming less monumental and more tender and gentle, especially with regard to the facial expression; it is this new approach, rather than any actual variation in the size or disposition of the figures, that shows the development of style from century to century throughout this Second Golden Age of Byzantine art.

The date of the mosaics in Sancta Sophia at Salonica has been disputed, but there seems every reason to believe that the Virgin in the apse—this time seated instead of standing—is to be assigned to around 886.[1] The Virgin replaced a cross which was set up during Iconoclasm, but when the change was made, much of the original background was left untouched, and there are even monograms still in position which refer to persons of the Iconoclast period. The conch of the apse is very severely curved, so that it is hard to secure a photograph of this mosaic that does not throw the Virgin very much out of proportion. Even so, the head is somewhat over large and the general effect far less impressive than at Nicaea, and the mosaic is less satisfactory from the artistic point of view than that in the dome of the same church which depicts the Ascension at the centre, with tall figures of the Apostles between trees below (Pl. 29). Diehl thought that it should be dated to the eleventh century, and others have favoured the tenth, but the style definitely argues against this date; some of the figures indeed almost suggest pre-Iconoclast art, and there is good reason to accept evidence put forward by Lazarev in favour of a date between 842 and 850.[2] The Apostles are tall and elongated and are poised above the soil in completely unearthly attitudes. The artist has in fact been carried away into a transcendental world of religious ecstasy, seeming to have forgotten that it was Christ alone who rose from the dead and that the Apostles were still alive at the time. In fact, we see here for perhaps the first time the final liberation of art from the straightforward

---

[1] Demus, *Byzantine Mosaic Decoration*, London, 1947, p. 53.
[2] *History of Byzantine Painting*, Moscow, 1947 (in Russian), II, pls. 41, 42 and 43.

narration of the Roman world into a sphere of poetic fantasy which was equalled at a later date only in the work of el Greco.

But Sancta Sophia at Salonica is not the only instance of such a comprehension, for now that Iconoclasm had been finally defeated, artists tended to treat every rendering of the saintly or religious form as an expression of faith; indeed, the decoration of the church interior as a whole was looked at in this way and appears to-day as a further manifestation of this preoccupation with the unworldly. Deep symbolism underlaid the decoration, and the interior of the church was conceived of as an expression of the triune nature of the universe, with heaven above, earth below, and paradise between. Portraits of bishops and the minor saints thus occupied the lower levels of the walls, angelic and divine figures were shown on the roofs and vaults, while the saints or the events from the Bible story were ranged in between, to bridge the gap between the celestial and the mundane worlds. The Apostles in the Ascension group at Salonica thus savour of the divine when associated with this scene of outstanding religious significance; when shown alone, as individuals, their depiction was usually permeated with the divine essence to a far lesser degree.

At the end of the ninth century the story can be taken up once more in Sancta Sophia at Constantinople, with a mosaic over the west door in the narthex; it depicts Christ enthroned, with the Emperor Leo VI (886 g/a) at His foot. It is of a much less transcendental character than the Salonica Ascension, owing partly to its disposition within the "mundane" sphere of the church and partly to its subject matter. The face of Christ is thus dignified rather than ecstatic, and expresses human sympathy rather than divine awe. An ivory of Christ in the Victoria and Albert Museum may be compared; it should be assigned to much the same date (Fig. 19). An archangel on the vault in front of the apse in Sancta Sophia illustrates a similar trend, though there is perhaps more classical influence and also more expression. It is a figure of outstanding elegance and beauty and is especially interesting in the way the curve of the vault was compensated for to give an effective view from the ground or the gallery. It is probably to be assigned around 900.[1]

---

[1] The apse mosaics have not yet been fully published, but see T. Whittemore in *The American Journal of Archaeology*, April-June 1942, p. 169, for a preliminary notice, and Demus, *op. cit.*, pl. 25, for a reproduction. For the other mosaics in Sancta Sophia see T. Whittemore, *The Mosaics of St. Sophia at Istanbul*, I, II, III and IV.

Fig. 19. Byzantine Ivory, Christ. Ninth century.
Victoria and Albert Museum, London.

Salonica. Sancta Sophia. Dome mosaic: the Ascension. Mid ninth century. (*Photo Lykides.*)

PLATE 29

(a) Ivory: the Virgin and Child.
Archaeopiscopal Museum, Utrecht.
Eleventh century. (*Photo Museum.*)

PLATE 30

(b) Painting on silk: St. Just.
Cathedral of St. Just, Trieste.
Eleventh century. (*Photo Giraudon.*)

(a) David between Wisdom and Prophecy, from psalter Vatican Palat. Gr. 381. Tenth century. (*Photo Vatican Library*)

(b) Nicaea. Church of the Assumption of the Virgin. Mosaic in pendentive of the dome: St. Mark. 1025–1028. (*After Schmidt.*)

PLATE 31

(a) The Monastery of Hosios Lukas, Greece. Mosaic: Incredulity of Thomas. Eleventh century. (*Photo Schultz.*)

(b) Constantinople. Sancta Sophia. Mosaic: the Zoe panel, 1028-1042 (*The Byzantine Institute.*)

PLATE 32

The next mosaic in point of date is in the southern vestibule of Sancta Sophia; it shows the Virgin between Constantine and Justinian. The approach is more prosaic and less interpretational than that of the preceding works; it is grand rather than moving. It is probably to be dated to the reign of Basil II (976-1025), who was noted as a patron of the arts as well as an able general under whom the frontiers of the empire were considerably extended. His name is associated with a Psalter, now in the Marcian library at Venice (Gr. 17, 421), which bears his portrait on the title page, with, on the next page, six scenes from the life of David (*Byzantine Art*, pl. 31). It is one of a number of fine manuscripts which are usually classed as the "aristocratic" group. A Copy of the Old Testament in the Vatican (Reg. Gr. 1), known as the Bible of Leo the Patrician, of the second quarter of the tenth century, and a Psalter in the Vatican (V. Palat. Gr. 381), of much the same date, are probably the most important examples of the group. Two masters worked on the first, one of whom followed a more painterly, the other a more linear style. The second was probably illustrated by a single master, who worked in the grand manner associated with the capital—the rendering of David between Wisdom and Prophecy is typical (Pl. 31, *a*). These grand and majestic paintings, for that is what they are, even though on a small scale, may be contrasted with the illustrations of another group of manuscripts which are adorned not with full page plates but with vivid little drawings in the margins. They are known as the "marginal" Psalters. The drawings are perhaps not great art, but they are vivid and expressive, at times almost verging on caricature.

If some of the illustrations in these manuscripts—and there are of course many others which it has not been possible to mention here—attest the survival or revival of a rather classical style, that style is to be seen very much more to the fore in secular art, and it was perhaps in this direction that Constantine Porphyrogenitus' love of the past had its most marked effect. The illustrations in a copy of the Theriaca of Nicandor in Paris (Bib. Nat. Supp. Gr. 247) are thus almost completely Pompeian, while the large group of ivory caskets already noted (p. 101) bear as their decoration scenes from classical mythology which, so far as iconography is concerned, might well be Hellenistic works of the second century A.D. But the style and the occasional presence of Christian themes of a fully developed Byzantine character make it possible to date these caskets to the tenth century. Examples of the group exist in numerous museums; the finest are probably the Veroli casket in the Victoria and Albert Museum and a rather similar one in the Cluny Museum in Paris (*Byzantine Art*, pl. 50).

The delicate but rather severe carving of the borders, which on these caskets almost invariably take the form of rosettes, may be compared with that on a number of ivories with religious subjects, where the same high degree of proficiency and the same very finished style are present. But if any ancient style is called forth for comparison, it is here not so much the picturesque outlook of the Hellenistic world as the selective brilliance of the Hellenic that is to the fore, and the carvings of this group are to be described as "neo-Attic". Constantinople was the main centre of the revival of this style, and works in this elegant, polished and delicate manner came into great favour there throughout the eleventh and early twelfth centuries.

Most are on a small scale, but happily a few pieces of stone sculpture survive which are in the same style, notably a battered but still very lovely bas-relief of the Virgin in the Museum of Antiquities at Istanbul which was found on the site of the Mangana Palace. Its formal lines, elegant balance and precise carving are typical of the best that the capital stood for in the so-called "Second Golden Age" of Byzantine art (Fig. 20). We see the same manner on a number of ivories which must also be assigned to Constantinople, and to the same date and the same workshops. Most outstanding is the plaque with the Madonna at Utrecht, already alluded to, which is one of the most lovely ivories that has ever been carved (Pl. 30*a*). But there are plaques closely related with Apostles upon them at Venice, Dresden and Vienna; there is a particularly fine ivory of St. John the Baptist at Liverpool, and there are three triptychs, of which the finest is that known as the Harbaville triptych in the Louvre, which may also be noted as typical of all that Constantinople stood for at this time. An ivory bearing the coronation of Romanos and Eudoxia by Christ—the Emperor is probably to be identified as Romanos II (c. 944)—is equally fine. Similar work was done in the eleventh century, but in its latest phase carvings of this group tended

FIG. 20. Marble sculpture from the Mangana Palace, Constantinople. The
Virgin Orans. Eleventh century. The Museum of Antiquities, Istanbul.

to slight exaggeration of the characteristics of elegance and delicacy and there was at times a touch of effeminacy in the work.

In painting the same rather cold, but grand and elegant manner appears, though examples are rare; a portrayal of St. Just on silk, now in the Cathedral of St. Just at Trieste, is perhaps the most striking example (Pl. 30, *b*). The inscription is in Latin and the work was probably done in Italy, but it is, in spirit, much more Byzantine than it is Italian.

None of the mosaics of the eleventh century—and quite a considerable number survive—shows this revival of "neo-Attic" characteristics to quite the same degree as do the carvings, though they are present none the less, as for example in a figure of the Virgin in the Orans position which stood in a lunette at Nicaea; it must have been set up between 1025 and 1028. The Evangelists, which occupied the four pendentives below the dome of the same church and which belong to the same date, are akin, and are imbued with a lovely, tender quality. They must have been some of the most outstandingly lovely mosaics of the age, for they combine grandeur and tenderness, dignity and sympathy in a particularly subtle manner (Pl. 31, *b*).

Of much the same date is the Zoe panel in the south gallery of Sancta Sophia at Constantinople. Christ is represented between the Empress Zoe (1028-57) and Constantine IX Monomarchos (1042-55) (Pl. 32, *b*). Now a technical examination of the mosaic proves that the head of this portrait is a restoration. It would seem that originally Zoe's first husband, Romanos III, was represented. A new head was put in and the name in the inscription was altered when she remarried, and at the same time her own head was redone, to be in keeping with that of Monomarchos. The mosaic as a whole would thus date from between 1028 and 1034, though the heads are later. The work, though grand and proficient technically, is somewhat cold and arid, and represents the "neo-Attic" tradition at its worst. Other mosaics of the eleventh century outside Constantinople —and one series of wall paintings also—are far more alive and more effective, and present what is probably a truer picture of Byzantine art at this time, even though they are not in Sancta Sophia, the hub of the Byzantine world.

The most complete series of these more expressive mosaics is in the larger of the two churches in the monastery of Hosios Lukas, not far from Delphi, in Greece. The decoration probably dates from the second quarter of the eleventh century. A complete cycle of the life of Christ once existed, but many of the scenes have now perished. Those that survive are very striking, notably the Incredulity of Thomas and the strangely expressive Crucifixion (Pls. 32, a and 33, a); the style is essentially an "expressionist" one, the figures are squat and dumpy and the iconography bears witness to an eastern heritage, which probably penetrated by way of Cappadocia. But, as in much eastern work, colour plays an important role, and the general effect of the decoration is profoundly spiritual. The Pentecost scene occupies the dome, the disposition being somewhat similar to that of the Ascension in Sancta Sophia at Salonica. It is one of the last instances where a scene of this sort appears in the main dome; in later churches this place was almost invariably reserved for Christ Almighty, as, for example, at Daphni near Athens.

Eastern in style again are the mosaics of the Nea Moni on the Island of Chios, which are to be dated between 1042 and 1056. The colouring here is even brighter and more striking than at Hosios Lukas, the facial expressions are extremely forceful, and the work as a whole shows a very personal touch, especially in small details. The artist, in fact, was a supreme master of the "expressionist" style. There may be tenderer renderings of the Descent into Hell—a very popular scene in Byzantine art from this time onwards—but there is certainly no more effective one than at the Nea Moni, and nowhere is the distinction between divine, saintly and mortal existence more clearly rendered. The scene occupies an apse; it is a magnificent composition in itself, and the personal style of the artist is to be seen in the curious expressions and heavily bearded or darkly shaded faces of those rising from the dead, in contrast to the more naturalistically rendered faces of the kings behind. The Washing of the Feet, which is also well preserved, is similarly expressive, and even the individual portraits in medallions show the same personal style. The sweeping way in which the highlights are treated, as for instance in a medallion bearing St. Anne, clearly heralds the style that was to be adopted in a great deal of later painting of the so called Cretan school; the manner is essentially painterly, and may be contrasted with the very linear way in which the high-lights are treated in the Zoe panel in Sancta Sophia at Constantinople.

To very much the same date are to be assigned the mosaics in Sancta Sophia at Kiev in Russia. Their style is however quite distinct, being harder and more linear, and lacking the painterly feeling and colourful treatment of Chios or Hosios Lukas. Much of the work at Kiev is in fact essentially provincial; that at Hosios Lukas and Chios, though distinct from what was being done at Constantinople, was personal and individual and the Chios master in particular was one of outstanding ability.

The last decoration of the eleventh century that must be considered is one that has already been mentioned briefly, namely that of Sancta Sophia at Ochrid in Macedonia; this time it is in paint, not in mosaic. The church, like so many in Greece and the Balkans, was turned into a mosque by the Turks, and the paintings were in part destroyed and in part covered over. The work of cleaning those that survive is still in progress, but what has been uncovered is enough to attest the very high quality and the great interest of these paintings. On historical grounds they can be assigned to the first half of the eleventh century. The subjects comprise a vast Dormition of the Virgin on the west wall (*Byzantine Art*, pl. 17) and a series of Old Testament scenes in the presbytery in front of the apse; those showing Abraham's Sacrifice are best known, thanks to the excellent colour reproductions in the Unesco volume on Yugoslavia. Others are no less fine, notably the procession of angels on the choir vault, moving towards the east to do homage to the Virgin in the apse. The figures show a wonderful command of rhythmical movement in the rendering of an old, hallowed and widely distributed theme. No less effective is the illustration on Jacob's dream (Pl. 34, *b*). The whole rendering is essentially imaginative, as such a theme demands, and if it is analysed logically seems strange, even incompetent; the angel is thus curiously out of proportion to the ladder on which it stands. But the small figure is extremely expressive; Jacob's face conveys the fact that he is in a trance, and the whole picture is profoundly expressive of the visionary outlook of the age.

The forceful style of all these works in paint and mosaic alike contrasts very markedly with the more delicate, classical outlook that we noted in some of the manuscripts at the beginning of the century and even more in ivories which must have been produced throughout the whole period. These were the works typical of all that the capital stood for, and on them should be based our ideas of the Constantinopolitan school. Its work was polished, finished and essentially "neo-Attic". The mosaics of Hosios Lukas and Chios and to a lesser extent the paintings of Ochrid show little of this style; it is the eastern, "expressionist" manner that is there to the fore, and manuscripts like the Leningrad Lectionary must have served as the models that inspired these artists, rather than the "aristocratic" Psalters of the Constantinople school.

As has been noted above, the Leningrad Lectionary was probably illustrated in Asia Minor (p. 106). Millet in his penetrating study of architecture in Greece and the Balkans,[1] has shown that the currents of influence that affected these areas in building methods and ideas had their main source in Asia Minor. Those that affected painting probably stemmed from the same source, and the influence of the Cappadocian wall paintings is certainly to be seen at Hosios Lukas. Salonica, on the other hand, would appear to have been linked fairly closely with Constantinople. It is possible that in the smaller places the links were always with the East, but it is impossible to dogmatise, for our picture is an incomplete one and in the twelfth century the situation appears in a rather different light, for then one series of mosaics, those at Daphni near Athens (c. 1110) and one series of paintings, those at Nerezi in Yugoslavia (1164), belong quite definitely to the Constantinopolitan family, and the same manner is to be seen in the mosaics of the church of St. Michael of the Golden Head at Kiev, done in 1108. These more elegant works of the twelfth century, which are in general in the style of the capital, and which bear out the evidence of the ivories, will be discussed in the next chapter.

BOOKS

O. Demus, *Byzantine Mosaic Decoration*, London, 1947.

E. Diez and O. Demus, *Byzantine Mosaics in Greece*, Cambridge, Mass., 1931.

[1] *L'Ecole grecque dans l'architecture byzantine*, Paris, 1916.

CHAPTER XII

THE TWELFTH CENTURY IN THE EAST

THE story of Byzantine art in the twelfth century may be begun—and ended—in Sancta Sophia at Constantinople, for though there are two series of mosaics elsewhere that belong to dates slightly earlier in the century than the first twelfth century mosaic in Sancta Sophia, the so called John panel, it was in the capital that the style that characterises this century was developed and from there that it spread to other places. And it was a fresh and very distinctive style, in which a new delicacy was to the fore and in which a new spirit of humanism slowly developed. These changes are, it is true, not very marked in the John panel, for though technically accomplished, it is not a work of very great artistic quality. But there are none the less hints of a change, firstly, in the attempt that was obviously made to present portraits that were true to life, and secondly in the way in which the high-lights were done in thin white lines, in a manner heralding that developed in icon painting in the fourteenth and fifteenth centuries. This is especially the case in the portrait of Alexios Comnenos, which is situated on a pier adjoining the John panel and which was in all probability done by the same mosaicist a few years later; it was set up in 1122. The John panel itself, which shows the emperor John II Comnenos (1118-43) and his queen Irene on either side of a somewhat rigid figure of the Virgin and Child, must have been set up about 1119, soon after he came to the throne. But even if the Virgin is rather rigid, her face is gentle and tender and the comprehension is quite distinct from that which we see at Hosios Lukas, in the Nea Moni on Chios, or in Sancta Sophia at Ochrid. She is already more personal and intimate, and the harsh "expressionist" manner of the earlier work has been cast aside.

This change is also clearly apparent in ivory carving; it is hinted at in the lovely ivory at Utrecht, which is probably still of the eleventh century; it is carried farther in that bearing the

The Crucifixion. (a) The Monastery of Hosios Lukas, Greece. Eleventh century. (*Photo Schultz.*)

(b) Daphni, Attica. *c.* 1100. (*Photo Demus.*)

PLATE 33

(*a*) Daphni, Attica. Dome mosaic: the Pantocrator. *c.* 1100.
(*Photo Talbot Rice.*)

(*b*) Ochrid. Sancta Sophia. Wall painting: Jacob's Dream. First half of the
eleventh century. (*Photo Hoddinott.*)

PLATE 34

Panel: Our Lady of Vladimir.   Twelfth century.   (*Tretiakov Gallery, Moscow*).

PLATE 35

PLATE 96

Daphni, Attica. Mosaic: the Transfiguration. *c.* 1100. *(Photo Talbot Rice.)*

Baptist at Liverpool or in a plaque in the Victoria and Albert Museum bearing a bust of St. John the Baptist in a medallion at the centre, and busts of Sts. Philip, Stephen, Andrew and Thomas in smaller medallions at the corners (*Byzantine Art*, pl. 54). The elegant "neo-Attic" style that characterised ivory carving in the eleventh century at the capital has here given place to a more delicate manner which at times approaches the effeminate and which is carried farther in a long series of small reliefs cut out of steatite, which seem to have become very popular at this time. Perhaps the soft stone and the rather soapy texture of the material exercised some influence on the change of style in carving, though the main cause of change was due to one of outlook rather than material.

The most extensive and important mosaic decoration of the age, even including what has survived at Sancta Sophia, is that at Daphni near Athens, which must have been executed soon after 1100. Here the change to the new manner has not gone very far, and the work is in a diversity of styles. The great Christ Pantocrator in the dome is thus still in an essentially "expressionist" manner, and the heavily bearded, strangely awesome figure savours of the eastern tastes and eastern ideas which we have already noted at Hosios Lukas (Pl. 34, *a*). It represents the very culmination of the "expressionist" style, and when softened down, as at Cefalu and Monreale, the result is far less effective. But most of the other compositions at Daphni are in a more restrained vein, and this becomes clearly apparent if the rendering of the Crucifixion there is compared with that at Hosios Lukas (Pl. 33). At the latter place the body of our Lord is contorted in agony, and the strange way in which the shading is executed and in which the muscles are indicated was obviously done to intensify the atmosphere of agony and horror. At Daphni the Virgin is calm and controlled, while St. John does no more than point out the figure of Christ, conceived as a symbol of the faith, while the figure of our Lord Himself is rendered as calm and static; the conception of His nature does not permit of pain or suffering; indeed, we see Him here as a figure that death could not touch. Not all the scenes at Daphni are as completely reticent as this one, but an atmosphere of sober calm prevails to a degree unprecedented in any decoration of the eleventh century; nowhere is this more clearly apparent than in the scene of the Transfiguration, which

L

occupies one of the squinches below the dome; it is expressive, but at the same time balanced and elegant (Pl. 36).

The development of this outlook can be traced in the next dated monument that we have, namely the mosaic decoration in the monastery of the Golden Headed St. Michael at Kiev, done about 1108. If these mosaics are compared with those in Sancta Sophia at Kiev, the change in style is obvious. The expressions are more tender in the younger and more pensive in the older figures, and where occasion demands there is a new liveliness in the faces, as for example in the figure of St. Demetrius. This important monument remains little known outside Russia; it deserves a very high place in the story of Byzantine art in the twelfth century, for it is still in the main a Byzantine monument, even if certain elements which are intrinsically Russian as opposed to Greek are already beginning to make themselves felt. But that the change which was to be carried forward on Russian soil was already incipient in the Byzantine world and not only developed in Russia or conceived of in the Russian mind alone, is shown most clearly if we look carefully at the panel known as Our Lady of Vladimir, now preserved in the Tretiakov Gallery at Moscow (Pl. 35).

This painting must have been executed by a Greek master who worked and had been schooled in Constantinople. It appears to have been taken to Russia about 1150 and must have been painted only a short time before. The more we learn of the style and nature of Byzantine art, the clearer does it become that an old suggestion that the panel should be assigned to the eleventh century must be discarded.[1] Style, understanding and iconography all support a later date. The theme, our Lady of Tenderness, itself attests the new outlook; the Child's face is pressed against that of its mother in human affection; she herself is an essentially personal figure, more the mother than the divinity; frontality has given place to a new three-quarter pose; the handling has lost many of the rigid conventions of an earlier age. If some of the older mosaics and paintings achieve their effect through grandeur, and others by

---

[1] A suggestion has recently been put forward that the surviving panel is a close copy of a twelfth century original done in the thirteenth century; see Konrad Onasch, "Die Ikone der Gottesmutter von Vladimir", in *Wissenschaftliche Zeitschrift der Martin-Luther-Universität*, Jahrg. V, Heft I, Halle, 1955, p. 55. There is something to be said for this theory, but on the whole a date around 1140 seems more probable.

means of exaggerations—what one may call dis-harmonies—
the painter of Our Lady of Vladimir achieved his effect through
sheer beauty. It is an essentially reverent, an essentially
Christian work; it would strike a beholder by the sheer sim-
plicity of its beauty, and quite apart from any other factors, it is
in this respect alone something of truly outstanding significance.

The humanism that we see here was carried farther in the
next dated work that has survived, the painted decoration of
the small church at Nerezi, near Skopolje in Macedonia. It was
executed in 1164 on behalf of a certain Alexis, a member of the
Comnene family, and the artist must have been a Constantinopolitan. He was a very accomplished master, who was capable
of interpreting the scenes of the New Testament story in a new
and very personal manner. The faces of the individual saints
show this. The older ones are loving and intimate; one could
tell them one's troubles and expect sympathetic understanding,
not merely admire them with awe from afar: the younger ones
are personal, characterful and alive. The protagonists in the
scenes of our Lord's life and Passion are human as much as
divine; the minor figures are vivid and dynamic. In the scene
of the Deposition (*Byzantine Art*, pl. 18), for example, Nico-
demus lets down the body with the tenderness of a father, while
the Virgin presses Christ's cheek to hers in a gesture of human
compassion. In the Lamentation she weeps as a mother would
weep, and the spectator is filled with feelings of human compassion in the way that he would be in the contemplation of a
picture from fifteenth century Italy (Pl. 37). There is a good
understanding of anatomy too, and the midwife in the Nativity
scene seems just to have stepped, with the vase she carries, out
of the Hellenic countryside. The colours are fresh, varied and
attractive. The heavy, somewhat sombre tones that dominated
in the paintings of Sancta Sophia at Ochrid have given place
to something more gentle, delicate and attractive; light blue
replacing dark in the backgrounds and bright colours sup-
planting the darker ones more usual in earlier work.

This manner is to be seen again in paintings in other parts
of the Byzantine world, more especially in Russia, where it was
rapidly developed by native masters after its introduction by
immigrant Greeks. Work in the church of the Saviour at Pskov,
dating from 1156, may be noted, but it has been much damaged
by restoration. More important is a group of Apostles in the

church of St. Demetrius at Vladimir, of 1195; they form part of a great composition of the Last Judgement. The Apostles are seated formally and frontally, in two tiers, but even if the arrangement is severe, the treatment of each individual figure is entirely personal, all are alive, there is great variety, and the faces are of outstanding beauty. Other work of the period in Russia is mostly in a more local style; for example, the paintings of the church of the Saviour Nereditsa, near Novgorod (1199). Some fragmentary paintings in the church of St. George at Staraya Ladoga, also of the second half of the twelfth century, are again in a local manner, though hints of the revival style that we see at Neresi in Macedonia are present also.

Outside Russia examples are less numerous. A mosaic depicting the communion of the Apostles, which was formerly at Serres in Macedonia, but which is now destroyed except for a fragment preserved in the church of St. George at Salonica, may be noted; it is probably to be assigned to much the same date as the Vladimir Last Judgement. The work is delicate, but there is less personal feeling, though this is probably to be attributed to the very individual hand of the Vladimir artist rather than to the conservatism of the mosaicist, for the way in which the high-lights are executed and the rather effeminate touch savour most definitely of the new style that began to dominate art soon after the middle of the twelfth century and which is usually termed that of the Byzantine Revival.

Not all the works of this age were in so advanced a style, however, and a few other mosaics which are to be assigned to the same or even to a rather later date are more conservative. Thus mosaics of the twelfth century in the monastery of Vatopedi on Mount Athos, two panels at Xenophontos on Mount Athos, and a composition showing Christ Pantocrator in the dome of the church of the Panaghia Parigoritissa at Arta, which may be as late as the thirteenth century, are essentially monumental in style and show little of the humanism or the lightness of touch that characterise the Nerezi paintings. The provinces must have moved very slowly behind the capital in the development of the new manner; though Nerezi is an isolated church in a distant area, it was the foundation of a patron of the imperial house, and its painter was, it would seem, a man from Constantinople, who had been schooled in the most advanced and up-to-date style.

The story of the development of the new style is, however, continued in other works of the later twelfth century: the most outstanding of them in point of quality is a mosaic showing the Deesis in Sancta Sophia at Constantinople (Frontispiece). There has been some argument as to the date of this panel. Whittemore, who was the first to publish it, assigned it to the early twelfth century, primarily on the basis of epigraphy, for the letters of the inscription that plays a prominent part in it are of a type which dominated at that time.[1] Subsequently it has been suggested that the lettering might belong to an older panel and that the figures or in any case the faces were redone at a later date. On that assumption they have been assigned to the late thirteenth or early fourteenth century on the grounds of similarities with the mosaics of Kahrieh Cami, which are firmly dated to around 1305. That a restorer would have redone the figures so elaborately and left the old inscription seems on the face of it very unlikely, yet the nature of the lettering would preclude a date as late as the end of the thirteenth century, were it and the figures contemporary. A more likely solution of the problem is that the inscription and the figures are contemporary, but that the inscription is not as early as Whittemore supposed. A date in the last quarter of the twelfth century thus seems most likely—one during the Latin domination of Constantinople (1204-58) would be most improbable.

Stylistic factors indeed support such a date. The Virgin is subtle and tender, yet still a figure of dignity; half-way, it would seem, between the rendering on the great dedication panel at Kahrieh, firmly dated to 1305,[2] and such a work as the Utrecht ivory, of the late eleventh century. The way in which the high-lights are indicated on the face of the Baptist recalls those of the Alexios portrait done in 1122, yet there is far more expression and feeling in the rendering. The figure of our Lord, though gentle, is rather more monumental than at Kahrieh. The blend of elements that we see here is similar, in fact, to that in the Virgin of Vladimir, and with it, the Sancta Sophia Deesis illustrates the summit to which painting achieved before the advent of the Crusaders in 1204.

It is, however, not only the quality of these works that is

[1] *Mosaics of Hagia Sophia*, Vol. IV.
[2] P. A. Underwood, "The Deesis Mosaic in the Kahrieh Cami at Istanbul", in *Late Classical and Early Mediaeval Studies in Honor of A. M. Friend*, Ed. K. Weitzmann, Princeton, 1955.

important in the history of art, but their nature and the humanist approach that they illustrate. For long it was held that this outlook was the prerogative of Italy, and that it was only as the result of the arrival on the scene of such men as Giotto that the old Byzantine manner, expressive or monumental as might be the case, was forsaken. Or it was again at one time held that works in the Byzantine world that showed such humanism should only be assigned to a late date; they were explained as due to the penetration of new ideas from Italy. Neither supposition is now tenable. Recent discoveries in the East have proved once and for all that the twelfth century Revival there was a fact that cannot be disputed.[1]

The innovations for which this Renaissance was responsible were carried farther in the Byzantine world in the thirteenth and fourteenth centuries, especially in Constantinople, in the Peloponnese, in Serbia and in Russia. But progress never went as far as in Italy, nor indeed could it have gone as far in a society where conservatism in religious art played so fundamental a part, and where patronage was so closely controlled by the church authorities. A Byzantine Leonardo is really unthinkable, though the Byzantine world could boast more than one Fra Angelico; indeed Andrew Rublev, the greatest individual painter that Russia has produced, is in many ways most closely comparable to him. Moreover, the Italian Renaissance, so far as it was looking backwards, had its source in the mundane, narrative art of Rome; if Byzantium looked back, it was to the colder, grander art of the Attic style. The two Renaissances are thus not really comparable; what it is essential to recognise is that the Byzantine one took place first and that the art it produced reached its highest apex in the twelfth, thirteenth and very early fourteenth centuries, whereas the Italian one hardly began till after 1300. When it did come it benefited to some extent from the Byzantine experiments, though in the main it sought other ends. The two had humanism in common, but Byzantine art remained none the less a religious art, governed by a basically transcendental outlook. Italian art rapidly became secularised, and even when it was done in the service of the church, the outlook was more material.

---

[1] Bettini is still not prepared to accept it, and dates the Deesis even later than Kahrieh; see "I Mosaici dell'Atrio di San Marco e il loro seguito", in *Arte Veneta*, VIII, 1954, p. 38.

And when, in the sixteenth century, it sought to return to its spiritual anchorage, the change had been accomplished so effectually and so completely that it was only on the very rarest occasions that it was able to do so. El Greco, thanks to his Byzantine upbringing and Greek outlook, was able to achieve the transition, and so to become a painter whose art was essentially transcendental. Rubens, on the other hand, was always a complete materialist and he never acquired, even if he sought, a truly spiritual art. The work of the Carracci, Caravaggio and their followers was, from the spiritual point of view, never more than an ill-assorted blend of religious themes and worldly outlook. Regarded as Christian art, it is completely without significance.

BOOKS

T. WHITTEMORE, *The Mosaics of Haghia Sophia at Istanbul*, Parts III and IV, London, 1942 and 1952.

G. MILLET, "L'Art Byzantin", in A. Michel, *Histoire de l'Art*, Vol. I, Paris, 1905.

CHAPTER XIII

BYZANTINE ART IN ITALY IN THE ELEVENTH AND TWELFTH CENTURIES

IT so happens that quite a number of the surviving Byzantine mosaics and even a few of the large-scale paintings of the twelfth century are to be found on Italian soil; they were the work either of Greek craftsmen loaned from Constantinople itself or of pupils whom they took on and taught in the locality where they were being employed. These works are to be distinguished from those of a basically Italian character, done by masters who had been born and who had learnt in Italy. Even if the latter show Byzantine influence, as they very often do, the influence is a deep-seated one, going back to an earlier date, and witnesses either the common origin of Byzantine and mediaeval Italian art or the close contacts that existed between the two areas right down to the time of the Turkish conquests. It must not be forgotten that when Byzantine power began to wane, the coastal cities of Italy took up the maritime trade, and Venice, Genoa, Pisa and other towns had their own quarters in Constantinople even before the time of the fourth crusade (1204). The results of these contacts will be considered in a subsequent chapter; here we are concerned with works that are essentially Byzantine, but happen to be on Italian soil.

We may begin with the earliest of them, on the extreme fringe of the country, namely the Cathedral of St. Just at Trieste. In the apse of the northernmost of the two parallel aisles that constitute the Cathedral is a mosaic showing the Virgin and Child flanked by St. Michael and St. Gabriel; below are figures of the Apostles, divided into two groups by a palm tree. The work was probably done in the eleventh century, but follows an earlier model fairly closely. The mosaics were restored in 1863, and the ensemble is to-day not of the very first quality. In the apse of the southern church our Lord is shown treading on the Asp and Basilisk, with St. Just on one side and San Servolo on the other. The work is Byzantine in style, but the subject is one which was more popular in western than in eastern iconography; it became very popular in this country from Norman times onwards. An interesting painting on silk, which has already been mentioned, is also preserved in the Cathedral; it once again represents St. Just (see p. 156 and Pl. 30, *b*).

The mosaics of St. Mark's at Venice are on a far more extensive scale than those at Trieste, for every square foot of the upper portions of the walls is covered. By no means all the mosaics are, however, to be counted as Byzantine; some are frankly Renaissance in style, and others are Latin rather than eastern, deriving from wall paintings like those of early Romanesque style in Rome, and ultimately from such works as the Italianate paintings in Sta Maria Antiqua rather than from the East. Taken as a whole, the mosaics of St. Mark's are not very satisfactory from the aesthetic point of view, in comparison with those of a purely Byzantine style, for the formalism entailed by the technique found itself in admirable accord with the wholly transcendental outlook of Byzantine art, but did not blend well with the more naturalistic outlook of Renaissance art in Italy. The Italianate portions of the work are in a rather wooden manner and lack the profundity of the best of the Byzantine; the expressions tend to be rigid, the figures clumsy, and the compositions do not fill the space they occupy in a fully satisfactory manner. In the Miracle of Moses in the porch, for example, the scene is crowded into the bottom of the picture, and there is a great space of sky above which seems empty and pointless; it does not serve to accentuate the grandeur and spirituality of the scene as is the case in the mosaic of the Virgin in the apse at Torcello (Pl. 38). How much more effective are the compositions of the scenes in the squinches at Daphni, where the vacant spaces are all vital to the composition as a whole and where the work is distinguished by perfect balance (Pl. 36). And in certain other instances at St. Mark's, where the bare background is filled in with a profusion of stars, as in the Ascension in the central dome, an even less satisfactory effect results. Though the stars are perhaps not noticeable in a general view, they certainly mar the effect if the central medallion is studied in detail. Nor do the figures between this medallion and the windows carry conviction; at times they seem rigid and static, at others the attitudes are awkward and difficult; the manner of Sancta Sophia at Salonica seems in fact to have been followed, but without understanding, and in nearly all the work at St. Mark's one feels that very worldly minds were trying to produce art of a basically spiritual character. Because the transcendental vision was foreign to their outlook, they resorted to symbols of the unworldly, like the stars in the dome, to achieve their result. But the symbols seem hollow and the pictures fall far short of those where spirituality was inherent, as at Daphni or Salonica. The mosaics in a purely Renaissance style are even less satisfactory, for their basic naturalism blends most unhappily with the formalism of the medium.

All these works were done around 1200, except for those in a Renaissance style, which are later, and though in the East some of the most lovely mosaics and wall paintings date from the thirteenth and fourteenth centuries, in the West the thirteenth century was, taken as a whole, an age of decadence, which was relieved by the birth of a completely new outlook around 1300, when Giotto came upon the scene. But there are other mosaics in St. Mark's of rather earlier date which are finer from the artistic point of view; most important of them are scenes from the life of our Lord and the Virgin in the nave. They are probably to be assigned to the early twelfth century; they cannot be dated before 1063, for the structure was only begun in that year. Their style is rather archaic but does not fail to carry conviction.

Of higher quality than the mosaics of St. Mark's are those in the simple but very lovely basilical church at Torcello, which was founded in 641 but completely rebuilt in 1008. The mosaics can be divided into three distinct groups, those in the main apse, those in the apse of the southern aisle, dedicated as the chapel of the Holy Sacrament, and those on the west wall. They are to be assigned to a diversity of periods. Those in the chapel of the Holy Sacrament belong to the mid twelfth century; they depict Christ, holding the Gospels, between the Archangels Michael and Gabriel, with, on the wall below, Sts. Nicholas, Ambrose, Augustin and Martin. The work is not very distinguished, the figures being rather squat and ill-proportioned and the stances somewhat wooden; the effect is distinctly provincial.

The rather heavy style of these figures is in marked contrast

to that which characterises the Virgin in the conch of the main
apse, a beautifully balanced, aetherial figure, supremely dignified, yet at the same time intimate and gentle. The way in
which this tall figure is silhouetted against the gold background
is one of the most outstanding artistic achievements of the age.
The conception of the figure is deeply spiritual and the understanding thoroughly Byzantine. The Apostles on the vertical
wall below also show good work, though the effect that they
convey is inevitably somewhat more prosaic. They are to be
dated to the early eleventh century and constitute a part of the
original decoration of the church; the Virgin above is probably
to be dated around 1190. It has been suggested that the figure
was substituted for one of Christ, no doubt contemporary with
the Apostles below. That the standing Virgin was a substitute
for an enthroned figure can be seen from a careful study of the
mosaic itself at close quarters. That this figure represented
Christ is supported by the evidence of iconography, for in the
eleventh and twelfth centuries in the Byzantine world a figure
of Christ was almost always included in any scheme of church
decoration. The correct place for such a figure was of course
the dome, as for example at Daphni, but where there was no
dome, as at Torcello, Cefalu and Monreale, Christ passed to the
apse. The inscription on the face of the apse also seems more
appropriate to Christ than to the Virgin. It reads:

"Sum Deus atque caro patris et sum matris imago,
    Non piger ad lapsum, sed fluentia proximus adsum."[1]

In contrast to the very spiritual rendering of the Virgin in
the apse is the wholly narrative conception of the great composition of the Last Judgement on the west wall. This composition was severely restored in the middle of the last century
and bits of the original work were extracted and are now preserved either in a little museum attached to the church or in
various collections outside the Venetian region. The style of
these fragments is alive and expressive, and though they were
copied fairly exactly by the restorers, the copies remained
somewhat flat and monotonous. In a very masterly study of
these mosaics Demus has pointed out the extent of these restora-

---

[1] "I am God and the flesh of the Father and the image of the Mother; not
slow to punish a fault, but at hand to aid those who waver."

tions and has also noted that parts of the original work were probably done by Greek workmen, whereas other parts show the harder, less sympathetic style which we see in St. Mark's and which is to be regarded as characteristic of Venice.[1]

A figure of the Virgin, as tall as that in the main apse at Torcello, and similarly isolated against a plain gold background, is preserved in the apse of the church on the neighbouring island of Murano. But though the proportions are effective, the detail of the face is less impressive, and there is a certain weakness in the rendering of the draperies. A miniature mosaic showing the Annunciation in the Victoria and Albert Museum may be compared. Both are probably to be assigned to the fourteenth century, a period at which these mosaics on a small scale, made of cubes no larger than a pin's head, set in wax, became very popular. Examples are preserved in a number of museums and treasuries in East and West alike.

On an even more extensive scale than those in and around Venice are the mosaics of Sicily, which were set up under the patronage of the Norman kings from just before the middle of the twelfth century onwards for some sixty years. In many cases they were the work of Greek masters. The earliest and probably also the best of them are at Cefalu. The Cathedral there is a basilical structure of great impressiveness and beauty, in a semi-Norman, semi-Arab style. It was begun in 1131, but the presbytery and apse were not finished till 1148, and the mosaics were added between then and about 1200, when the vaulted roof was completed. Those in the apse itself seem to have been done immediately on the completion of the structure. Owing to the absence of a dome, the figure of Christ is here placed in the conch of the apse, the next most important position in the church and the nearest to the "heavenly" as opposed to the "earthly" zone. The Virgin, who should normally occupy the conch, has been pushed down to the highest register of the vertical wall. On either side of her are two very impressive winged archangels, and below her a window, with on either side of it the twelve Apostles, in two registers. The figure of Christ is particularly beautiful; more tender and more sentimental than the one at Daphni, but still impressive and grand

---

[1] Demus, "Studies among the Torcello Mosaics", *Burlington Magazine*, Vol. 83, 1943, pp. 136 ff., and Vol. 84, pp. 41 ff. and pp. 195 ff.

and at the same time deeply poetic in feeling; some of the details, notably the hands, are outstanding (Pl. 39). The text of the Bible our Lord holds is half in Greek, half in Latin, and is thus admirably adapted to the semi-Greek, semi-Latin civilisation of Sicily at the time. But the workmanship of this mosaic must have been Greek, even if in other places in the Island a more prosaic trend indicates that locally trained pupils had taken over from their Byzantine masters.

The mosaics of the presbytery leading to the apse are probably rather later; Demus suggests a date around 1160, Lazarev one as late as 1230. The former seems more probable. On the vault are two cherubim, two seraphim and four angels, forming a very striking decorative composition, and on the walls are scenes in four registers.

It is to be questioned whether any of the other mosaics of Sicily are quite as fine and quite as impressive as those of Cefalu, though in the Palatine chapel at Palermo there is a much fuller and more complete decoration, and in the Church of the Martorana in the same town the work has a soft, delicate charm which is very much its own, and which is absent in the more impressive church of Cefalu. The Martorana was founded, built and endowed in 1143 by George of Antioch, and the mosaics were finished by about 1148. Unlike the rest of the buildings of Sicily, the church took the form of a Greek cross, with a dome at the centre and a transverse narthex at the west end. It was thus a completely Byzantine structure. Its plan survives, but the whole eastern arm has been redecorated in the Sicilian rococo style and looks singularly out of keeping with the rest. Mosaics, however, survive in the northern, southern and western arms of the cross, and also in the narthex, where there are two interesting dedicatory panels showing Christ crowning King Roger II and the Admiral George of Antioch prostrated before the Virgin. In the body of the church the Gospel story is told in a series of scenes. The inscriptions are in Greek, and the decoration must once more have been due to Greek masters. The new more humanistic approach which characterises the art of this age in the Byzantine world is apparent, for example in the way in which the Child Christ stretches out His arms to St. Simeon in the Presentation scene, which occupies the two triangular spaces over the western arch of the central vault, or in the realism of the scene of the Washing of the Child in the Nativity. In both He is represented as a real and lively infant, not as an ageless divine figure, of symbolic character. The effect is vivid, but the deeply spiritual understanding of such a picture as that of Our Lady of Vladimir is not quite achieved here, and one might say that these mosaics are charming rather than inspired. The rather unusual colouring, where pale greens, palish blues and pink predominate, bears out this impression. The decoration is delightful, but it does not achieve great profundity.

In spite of its completely Arab roof and of the fact that its mosaics are of several distinct periods, the decoration of the Palatine chapel is on the other hand perhaps more fully imbued with this character. The work at the eastern end, below the dome, is the earliest and best; it is dated to 1143 by an inscription; that in the nave was set up under William I after 1158; all was finished before 1189, though the mosaics have subsequently suffered from repeated restorations. A medallion of Christ Pantocrator occupies the dome in the usual way, but the figure is less impressive than those at Daphni and Cefalu owing to the overcrowded composition of archangels that surrounds it. Below, on the vaults and walls is a complete cycle of New Testament scenes, with inscriptions in Greek. Much of the work, though not perhaps all of it, must have been done by Greek craftsmen. In the nave there is an even more extensive Old Testament cycle, but here the inscriptions are in Latin and the work tends to be wooden and monotonous; these mosaics were undoubtedly done by the Sicilians whom the Greek immigrants had taken on as assistants and who eventually became masters in their own right.

If the Sicilians learned the art of mosaic from the Greeks, they were probably also indebted to them for what they did as painters, though here again the local work was rather less inspired and visionary. Two panels, each bearing the Madonna, may be noted as examples of their work. One is in the Metropolitan Museum at New York and the other in the Kahn collection. If they are compared with Our Lady of Vladimir, the characteristics that distinguish them as Sicilian works at once become apparent. In the one subtle tones, delicate handling and poetic understanding contrast markedly with the hard gold high-lights, the severe outlines and the distinctly prosaic touch of the others. Both Metropolitan and Kahn

Madonnas have been by some assigned to Constantinople,[1] but the technique and style is not such as should be associated with the Byzantine capital. It approaches much more closely to the manner of the nave mosaics of the Palatine chapel, and there is good reason to assign these panels to Sicily.

Progress—or regress it should perhaps be termed—was accentuated with the turn of the century, and the mosaics of Monreale, which date from the last quarter of the twelfth, if not from the early thirteenth century,[2] show it all too clearly. This is much the most extensive decoration in the island. The church is a really large cruciform basilica, and all its walls are completely covered with mosaics; it is in fact the largest single extent of mosaic that has survived either in East or West, but it is in other respects disappointing. The great Christ in the apse is very definitely a "copy" of the one at Cefalu; that is to say, the disposition and so forth are identical, but the work lacks the sparkle and fire of an original. The Virgin, Archangel and Apostles on the vertical walls of the apse are similarly uninspired when looked at carefully, though the general effect is impressive.

The figures in the apse represent the earliest work at Monreale; the extensive series of the Miracles of Christ, the Passion scenes and the Old Testament scenes in the nave were done next, beginning at the top at the east and ending at the bottom at the west. They are all on a large scale, and include a greater number of figures than was usually the case; in the Betrayal, for example, there are as many as thirty-one figures, excluding our Lord and Judas; elsewhere usually only five or six are shown at most. This profusion was the result of the size of the panels, which, like the building, are far larger than elsewhere. The same is true of the scenes in the side apses and transepts, which were probably done last. In all the scenes, especially those of the Old Testament, the narrative is vigorous and expressive; it is in the detail and in the liveliness of the individual figures that these mosaics fall short, as well as in the colouring, which is less rich and varied than at Cefalu, less distinctive than in the Martorana. The work must all have been

[1] For example by Berenson, *Studies in Mediaeval Painting*, Oxford, 1930. One is reproduced by Demus, *Byzantine Mosaic Decoration*, pl. 32, a.
[2] Work was begun about 1175, when the building was completed. Demus thinks it was all completed by the end of the century. Lazarev questions its unity, and assigns much of it to as late as 1230.

done by Sicilian craftsmen. Its patron was William II, who sought to transfer thither the Archbishopric. His reasons, it would seem, were primarily political, and this note of worldly expediency seems to ring through the whole edifice and its decoration. It was built and decorated for mundane aims, not because of faith—and Byzantine art is essentially an art of faith and exaltation.

Other work in Sicily, in the palace of the Ziza or the Norman stanza in the Palatine Palace, is secular. It is in a decorative, oriental style and falls outside the story of Christian art. Nor do a few small-scale decorations in the Byzantine style at Messina in Sicily and other places in Italy call for much more than a mention in a survey which is essentially general.

BOOKS

O. DEMUS, *The Mosaics of Norman Sicily*, London, 1949.

O. DEMUS, *Die Mosaiken von san Marco in Venedig, 1100-1300*, Baden bei Wien, 1935. A much fuller study in English is in preparation by the same author.

Nerezi, Macedonia. Wall painting: the Lamentation. 1164. (*Photo Ljubinković.*)

PLATE 37

Torcello.   Apse mosaic: the Virgin and Child and Apostles.
Eleventh and twelfth centuries.   (*Photo Alinari.*)

PLATE 38

Cefalu.   Apse mosaic: the Pantocrator, and below, the Virgin, Archangels
and Saints.   *c.* 1148.   (*Photo Alinari.*

PLATE 39

(a) Rome. Sta Maria Antiqua. Wall painting: Archangel. Seventh century. (*Photo Anderson.*)

(b) Mileševa. Wall painting: Angel, from the scene of the Marys at the tomb. c. 1234. (*Photo Ljubinković.*)

PLATE 40

Part V

LATER BYZANTINE ART

Though later Byzantine art was by no means as static as the authorities once asserted, it was, nevertheless, a very conservative style in comparison with those of the West, and its later manifestations, of fifteenth century date, are in many ways far closer to early Christian works in style and iconography than were the Romanesque works of the eleventh century. For this reason a final section, dealing with the last phase of Byzantine art, from the thirteenth to the sixteenth century, has been included, though in the West the story is not carried far beyond the year 1000. It might logically be argued that Russian art, which is essentially of the Byzantine family, should also have been considered. But Russian characteristics became marked at an early date, and the story of Russian art is really a new one which starts around 1300, and not the tail-end of an old. A chapter on icon painting has however been included, for though the panel paintings are iconographically and stylistically very closely related to wall paintings, they have usually been studied apart and, being portable, have an interest for collectors which the wall paintings have never achieved.

M

CHAPTER XIV

PAINTING IN THE BALKANS FROM THE THIRTEENTH TO THE SIXTEENTH CENTURY

IN 1204 the fourth crusade, instead of pushing forward to combat the infidel in Palestine, turned its energies to the conquest and sack of Constantinople, and for the next half-century the Byzantine capital was ruled over by Latin sovereigns. It is unlikely that any work of consequence in the artistic line was put in hand during that period. Members of the Byzantine imperial family, however, succeeded in escaping to the East and set up independent orthodox states at Nicaea and Trebizond. At the same time in the West, in the Balkans, new states were rising up which, even if they were not Greek, were none the less essentially Byzantine in culture, while on the mainland of Greece local "despots" also performed an important role as patrons. There have come down to us in all these areas, except Nicaea itself, a number of very remarkable paintings, and it is thus on the periphery rather than at the centre that artistic developments in the thirteenth century must be studied. But these works are all paintings; there were no mosaics in these areas, there was but little sculpture, and except for some fine embroideries the minor arts are all unimportant.

It was at Nicaea that the Greek Emperors first rallied against the Latin threat and from there that they returned to Constantinople in 1258. Nothing, however, now survives from this period in the city which was for some fifty-four years the main centre of Byzantine life and culture. It is now little more than an insignificant Turkish village and now contains no Byzantine remains other than the city walls. At Trebizond, on the other hand, where an independent Comnene dynasty ruled until 1461, quite a number of paintings survive, though most of them are of the fourteenth and fifteenth rather than the thirteenth century. Only those in the church of Sancta Sophia, a mile or so outside the town, are perhaps of earlier date. To judge from the little that is visible, they appear to be in a lively, rather naturalistic and definitely original style, which suggests that work of real quality was produced in Trebizond from soon after 1204, if not before. In the fifteenth century the influence of Constantinople is to be distinguished quite clearly in much of the work, for example that in the caves of St. Savas. It would seem, however, that there were then, and probably at an earlier date also, two distinct manners, the one eastern, inspired from Anatolia, the other more narrowly Byzantine, that is to say, Constantinopolitan; work of the former type is to be seen in the monastery of Sumela, where there are paintings closely akin to those in the rock-cut churches of Cappadocia.

The Trebizond paintings, though interesting, are unfortunately very fragmentary and appear at a disadvantage beside the much more extensive and better preserved decorations that have come to light in recent years in Serbia and Macedonia. Here a whole series of decorations on a very extensive scale are preserved in good condition, and they illustrate the gradual development of a distinctive Serbian school. The same is also true of Bulgaria, where a good deal of work is preserved, though it is perhaps rather more Greek and rather less national than that on Serbian soil. But even in Serbia, in spite of the progressive growth of the new national style, there were constant links both with Constantinople and with Greek Macedonia, and quite a number of the painters who worked in Slav Macedonia and southern Serbia were actually Greeks who at one time did decorations in Greece for Greek patrons and at another worked over the border for Slavs. What they did was of great interest, but none of the work is of quite as high a quality as that done by painters of Serbian birth in a number of churches which were set up and decorated under the patronage of members of the Nemandja dynasty. In these the older masters usually worked in the main body of the church, the younger ones in the narthices, and the young men tried out new themes and new ideas in a far more daring way than was ever the case in Greece.

The first distinctive Serbian paintings were those of the school of Raška, which was flourishing throughout the twelfth and thirteenth centuries; a culmination was reached at Studenica in the twelfth century, which is regarded by Radojčić as one of the first monuments of truly Serbian art.[1] But the finest and most impressive developments appear not so much at Studeniča as in a number of other monuments, of which Mileševa (1235), the central church at Peć (1250), Morača (1252) and Sopoćani (c. 1260) are the most outstanding.

Even a study conducted primarily on the basis of iconography would perhaps serve to indicate something of the strongly Serbian bias of the paintings at these places, but it is really the style, and more particularly the colouring, that shows it most clearly. Thus for the first time in the story of wall painting the backgrounds at Mileševa were coloured gold, and at Sopoćani the gold was criss-crossed in black lines to imitate mosaic cubes. This in some ways betokens a conservative outlook, the object being imitation of a hallowed medium, but in other ways it indicates experiment, for the practice had never been followed in Greece or the Byzantine world, though it appears again from time to time in Serbia. This blending of old and new is in fact typical, and the nature of the figures at Mileševa illustrates the same tendency. Thus the figure of the Angel at the Tomb is very classical, recalling the best of the work in Sta Maria Antiqua at Rome (Pl. 40), but the way in which the idea of the Risen Christ is indicated by a mummy suspended in space is something distinctly original. The facial character of the figures is again very distinctive.

The debt to work of the Byzantine Revival as exemplified by such paintings as those at Nerezi is quite obvious, but links with the West are also to be distinguished. As Radojčić has pointed out, the face of one of the young Apostles in the Assumption is so closely similar to that of the St. John in one of Giunta Pisano's Crucifixions that some sort of connection is indicated. Whether the Italian was inspired by this or a similar Serbian work, or whether the Serbs working at Mileševa had seen some of Giunta's paintings and were following his style, is, however, a question which cannot yet be answered. Both solutions are possible, for on the one hand the debt of the early Italians to the Byzantine world was considerable, while on the other the western elements in Serbian art became more and more important as time went on. It was perhaps the presence

---

[1] Xyngopoulos, on the other hand, suggests that Greek masters worked there; see *Thessalonique et la peinture macédonienne*, Athens, 1955, p. 24. Radojčić's view is here probably the correct one.

of these western elements that constitutes the most distinctive feature of the Serbian school. The royal portraits which play a prominent part in the decorations of nearly all the churches perhaps also owe their popularity to some extent to western ideas. Many of them are extremely effective, and the fine portrait of the founder at Mileševa, King Vladislav, is a very delightful picture as well as, obviously, a characterful portrait (Pl. 41, a).

These paintings, which are situated in the main body of the church at Mileševa, represent the Court school. They were done by three men whose names have come down to us, namely George, Demetrius and Theodore; they were presumably Serbs, for the inscriptions are in Slavonic. It has been suggested that this practice of recording the names of the painters is to be counted as another Serb, or perhaps rather Balkan, characteristic, for we find it also in Macedonia, though in Greece, for example at Mistra as late as the fourteenth and fifteenth centuries, the painters remain anonymous. Xyngopoulos has, however, argued that this was not universal in Greece, and he cites names from the southern Peloponnese to support his thesis.[1] The fact is that an interest in the personality of the painter was growing at this time along with the new humanism in art. But the Greeks remained more true to the old ideas than the Slavs, and in out of the way regions even in Serbia, where work of a less accomplished type was being done, the painters also usually chose to remain anonymous. This is true of the exo-narthex at Mileševa, which is in a far more primitive and less progressive style. It was perhaps done by local monks rather than professional painters of the Court school.

A rather similar primitive style characterises the earliest work at Peć, that in the central church. Here the backgrounds are dark blue, and the atmosphere gloomy and oppressive in contrast to the brilliance of Mileševa or the veritable gaiety of the colouring at Sopoćani. The rather ascetic character of the work at Peć is probably to be attributed to the personality of the artist who did it, for individual personality seems to have been allowed to express itself far more freely in Serbia than in the Greek world (Pl. 42). In any case the gloom of the Peć paintings is completely at variance with the greater brilliance and liveliness of those at Morača, done only two years later in

---

[1] Xyngopoulos, *op. cit.*, pp. 26 and 68.

1252. But even if the Peć paintings are sombre, the figure of Christ is extremely impressive and deeply moving.

The master of Morača seems to have been a good deal more sure of himself than were the men who worked in the narthex at Mileševa, but his style was rather more rhythmic and formal, and he used high-lights profusely. His style is also less distinctively Serbian than that of the Mileševa painter and much less so than that of the man who worked some ten years later at Sopoćani.

Sopoćani is perhaps to be regarded as the greatest masterpiece of Serbian art. The scenes are particularly vivid, being unusually full, with a mass of figures in them. The conception is, moreover, bold and the compositions grand and stately, though vivacious. The modelling of the faces is also very accomplished, and in most of them the effect is achieved by building up in warm tones on a green ground without using the white high-lights so much favoured by the Greeks. But it is the colouring that is the most distinctive feature at Sopoćani, and the masterly way in which curious tints of purple, green, blue and ochre are blended and the high-lights picked out in reflexes of different tones is not paralleled elsewhere. And if no individual figures to equal those of the Angel at the Tomb or the Virgin of the Annunciation at Mileševa are to be found,[1] the grouping at Sopoćani, as for example in the great composition of the Dormition, is unequalled elsewhere.

Quite a number of painters must have been engaged there, however, for not all the work is in the same style. Thus the full series of scenes from the story of Joseph is in a coarser manner; the heads are heavy and the proportions less elegant, and the general approach is more didactic. The style is in fact rather similar to that of Italian art of the thirteenth century; it suggests the manner of the contemporaries of Cavallini, and Okunev thinks that an Italian model was perhaps followed. Distinct again is the style of the portraits associated with the tomb of Anne, Mother of Uros, to be dated to 1264 or 1265. Though the proportions of the figures are strange and exaggerated, the faces are unusually expressive and personal for work of this period (Pl. 41, b).[2]

[1] Unesco, *Yugoslav Mediaeval Frescoes*, pls. xii and xiii. The colour plates in this book are excellent.

[2] Petković, "La Mort de la Reine Anne à Sopoćani", *Art Byzantin chez les Slaves*, I, p. 217.

Whether the paintings of Sopoćani were surpassed, or even equalled, in other decorations undertaken by artists of the Court school in the later thirteenth century we shall never know, for the monuments have perished. But with the fourteenth century a change to a more minute manner set in. It can be traced in a number of monuments which have nearly all been discovered only in the last ten years or so. Most important of them is the decoration of the body and outer narthex of a church at Prizren, called the Bogoroditsa Ljeviška. The work in the narthex is signed by a painter called Astrapas and was done between 1307 and 1309; that in the church is of the same date but probably by a different painter. The colouring is deeper, more naturalistic than at Sopoćani, the curious reflexes and subtly blended tones giving way to bolder, more contrasting colours; the interest in the subject matter is more intense, the modelling is more realistic and the figures are more natural. Especially significant is the way in which the various scenes are adapted to the wall space available. For example, the Communion of the Apostles is fitted very subtly above the most easterly of the arcades of the central aisle (Pl. 43). The conception is, in fact, less imaginative and aetherial, more straightforward and mundane. But the work is at the same time full of a profound sincerity and a desire to express the ideas of faith, though the means of expression are more limited in scope. Thus in the paintings in this church at Prizren it is the colours and the details of scenes and individual figures that are most effective rather than the great compositions, as at Sopoćani. In the narthex the most beautiful and expressive work is to be seen in the details; sections of outstanding beauty can be extracted from the larger compositions; one of the most outstanding is a rendering of the Crucifixion, only about two feet high. The grand tradition, exemplified in early times by the great Dormition of the Virgin on the west wall of Sancta Sophia at Ochrid, and in the thirteenth century by the rendering of the same scene at Sopoćani, now gives place to a new, more detailed manner, a development parallel to that which took place in Greece when the school called by Millet the Cretan came into being. But in Serbia the paintings are more impressive; in Greece they are perhaps more poetic.

Though he recognises the role played by Astrapas as an individual in bringing about this change in Serbia, Radojčić

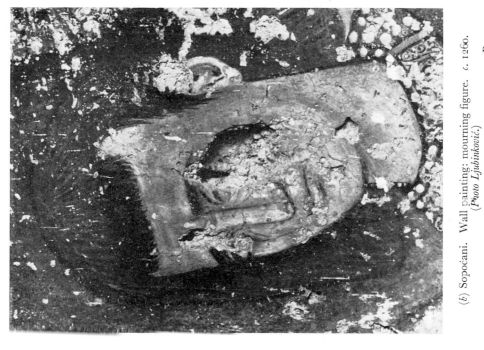

(a) Mileševa. Wall painting: portrait of the founder, King Vladislav. *c.* 1234. (*Photo Ljubinković.*)

(b) Sopoćani. Wall painting: mourning figure. *c.* 1260. (*Photo Ljubinković.*)

PLATE 41

Peć. Church of the Holy Apostles. Wall painting in apse: the Deesis. Fourteenth century. (*Photo Hoddinott.*)

PLATE 42

Prizren. Church of the Bogoroditsa Leviška. Wall painting; the Communion of the Apostles. *c.* 1307. *Photo Radojčić.*

PLATE 43

(b) Mistra, Peloponnese. The Brontocheion. Wall painting: the Prophet Melchizedek. *c.* 1360. (*Photo Talbot Rice.*)

(a) Boiana, near Sophia. Wall painting: Christ blessing. 1259. (*After Grabar.*)

PLATE 44

(p. 23) suggests that the change was also influenced by developments that were taking place at Constantinople. But the mosaics and paintings of Kahrieh Cámì stand somewhat apart, and with the exception of the Bogoroditsa Ljeviška at Prizren, there is little in Serbia that is closely similar. Nor is the work at Bogoroditsa Ljeviška at all close to any of that at Salonica, or indeed to any of the other important examples of the work of the "Macedonian" school.

This school is best represented in Slav Macedonia by the work of two other painters whose names we know, namely Michael and Eutychios. They signed the decorations] in the churches of St. Clement at Ochrid (1295) and St. Nikitas near Skopolje (1307-20), as well as that in the monastery at Staro Nagoričino (1317). At Ochrid the name of the former is coupled with that of Astrapas, but the style of the work there is absolutely distinct from that in the Bogoroditsa Ljeviška. Michael and Eutychios were essentially Macedonian painters, their work being closely similar to that of Panselinos in the Protaton on Mount Athos, and to that in the chapel of St. Euthemios in the church of St. Demetrius at Salonica (see p. 196). Their colours are more sombre and their figures larger; there is great liveliness, and even the saints have the appearance of portraits modelled on life. Again, every inch of wall space tends to be covered, so that the general effect is one of fullness. This is very much the case in St. Clement at Ochrid, where there is a complete series of New Testament scenes, as well as of full-length saints below. The signatures of the artists appear on the weapons, belts or other portions of the costumes; in St. Clement at Ochrid, for example, Michael's name is on St. Mercury's sword.

More important than Ochrid is the work at Staro Nagoričino (1317), where there is a very full decoration. The backgrounds are very detailed, with elaborate architectural compositions behind each scene, the compositions are balanced and impressive, and the narrative vivid. The figures tend to be angular, rather than suave (as at Sopoćani), in order to accentuate the dynamic effect.

The various decorations done around 1320 in the great monastery churches like Dečani (c. 1314) or Studeniča show the influence both of the Macedonian school, with the painters Michael and Eutychios at its head, and of the more purely

Serbian style, which we saw developing at Mileševa and Sopoćani. Much of the work has a rather literary character which was intensified by the habit of including quite lengthy texts or descriptive writings on the paintings; in earlier times the title of the scene was the most that was present. These descriptive legends were no doubt especially necessary at this time, for the churches of the period tended to be large, and the decorations, covering every square inch of wall-space, drew on apocryphal and unusual themes for their subject matter, so that without the inscriptions many of the scenes would have been obscure or unrecognisable.

Nowhere is the multiplicity of scenes that constituted the decoration of the later churches better exemplified than at Dečani done about 1335; Radojčić thinks the painters belonged to a school linked with the Adriatic as well as with the Byzantine world; others dispute these western contacts; they are certainly not very important. The complexity of the decoration is best indicated by figures; the Genesis story is represented by forty-six scenes, the Passion by forty-three, and the church calendar has no less than three hundred and sixty-five scenes. Though of outstanding interest from the point of view of iconography, the effect is somewhat overwhelming and monotonous from the artistic point of view, and only occasionally are the individual scenes really good. The same is true of the paintings of the large church at Gračanica. Here and there the details are good, and some of the figures are outstanding; for example, the head of St. John the Baptist in the conch of the northern side-apse is perhaps the most beautiful of all the fourteenth century paintings in Serbia (Pl. 46, a). But taken as a whole, Gračanica is rather disappointing, and the dream-like quality of the exterior of the church is not carried through in the interior. The heavy square piers that support the dome take up too much space, and the interior is unduly tall in comparison with the floor space available. The style of the work is Serbian, but the inscriptions are in Greek; as Greek was the accepted ecclesiastical language at the time, this is not really surprising.

During the greater part of the fourteenth century, probably as a result of unfortunate political relationships with Constantinople, Serbian art was not much refreshed by new ideas from Byzantium; what was new came, as often as not, from the West. On the whole, however, the tendency was towards greater

monotony and aridity. The extensive decorations of the church
of Milutin at Studenica and of the side churches at Peć are of
this type.

Developments in Macedonia took a rather different course,
for the country was less prosperous and only village churches,
rather than the large monastic institutions of Serbia, were
decorated. Towards the end of the fourteenth century an
intensely local school was working around Prilep under the
influence of the Metropolitan John. The iconography was
conservative, the style minute and better suited to panel
painting than to wall decoration, though a certain amount of
good work was done, notably in the monastery of St. Andrew
on the river Treska in 1389. Some of it had a vivid brilliance,
but in general these paintings lacked elegance and refinement.
Some of the figures were almost caricatures, like that of
St. Blaise at Marko Monastir done between 1370 and 1375.
But the scenes were often extremely expressive, like that
at the same place showing Rachel lamenting over her children.
The most extensive of these monastic decorations was that at
Lesnovo done in 1349, where Psalm 150, "O praise God in his
holiness", is illustrated on the walls for the first time; it was
previously known only as a subject for the illustration of
manuscripts.

Paintings which quite often showed real quality continued
to be produced here and there in out of the way places for a
century or so, but the last effective school of Serbian art was
that of the Morava valley, where the main resistance to the
advance of Islam was put up. The churches themselves were tall
and graceful, and the paintings inside them were characterised
by a delicate, refined and at times almost sentimental style,
akin to that of the so-called Cretan school in Greece (see p. 202).
Indeed, the decorations are really to be classed among the
works of the Cretan school. The figures were similarly tall and
elegant and stress was laid on a contemplative outlook, which
perhaps reflected the unsettled state of the times, the only
escape from which was to be found in the adoption of a
secluded monastic life. Typical of this school are the decorations
at Ravanića (1377), Ljubostinja (end of fourteenth century),
Kalenić (1405-10), Rudenića (1403-10) and Manassija (also
called Resava) (1407). Kalenić is perhaps the most important,
the paintings comprising an elaborated cycle from the life of

the Virgin. The same model, based on an apocryphal text, was followed here as in Kahrieh Cámì at Constantinople, but Kahrieh showed a more artistic, Kalenić a more literal and truly narrative, interpretation of it. A rare scene which appears at both is that of the Numbering of the People. The colouring at Kalenić also recalls Kahrieh, for it is very brilliant and daring. Shading is used very freely—more freely actually than at Kahrieh.

The essentially religious paintings at Kalenić may be contrasted with the founder portraits at Manassija, where some of the best work of this type of around 1400 is to be found, for after the Turkish conquests but little work of quality was done. The only church of these later times that deserves notice is indeed that of Poganovo, on the Serbo-Bulgarian frontier, which was painted about 1500. A good deal of Italian influence is to be noted there, for example in the costumes, the absence of bearded figures and so on; the painter was seeking to leave the Byzantine tradition in favour of something new, but had not sufficient competence to do so satisfactorily.

The story of painting in Bulgaria followed on broad lines the same course as that in Yugoslavia, that is to say there was a Byzantine core, on to which later national developments were grafted. But in early times this core showed closer links with the East, and at a later date closer links with Constantinople than was ever the case in Yugoslavia, and the Bulgarian style was also on the whole much more conservative than the Serbian. Though Slav inscriptions began to supplant Greek ones soon after the revival of the Bulgarian empire in 1186, local styles in painting like those that we see in Serbia never developed to the same degree. The fourteenth century paintings at such places as Tirnovo thus remain much more Greek than those at Bogoroditsa Ljeviška or at Dečani. One of the reasons for this is certainly to be found in the absence of western contacts. In Serbia we see the results of the action of the locality, the Serb blood of the painters, and that of western influence, upon the Byzantine foundation; in Bulgaria the western influence was absent, and the outlook of the Bulgars was itself different from that of the Serbs, and when influences from outside were exercised on the developing Bulgarian art, they stemmed in the main from Constantinople and not from the West or from other Byzantine centres where art had developed along its own lines.

The influence of Salonica and the Macedonian school, so important in southern Yugoslavia in the early fourteenth century, was thus never exercised in Bulgaria to the same degree.

The earliest paintings in Bulgaria that survive are a few fragmentary scenes in the eastern section of the church at Boiana near Sofia, in a style rather similar to that of the mosaics at Hosios Lukas. They are in bright colours, against a turquoise blue ground, and probably date from between 1018 and 1086. But the main decoration at Boiana, which overlies this early work except in a few places, was done on behalf of the Sevastocrator Kaloyan in 1259. It comprises a very full cycle of New Testament scenes, both in the eastern section of the church and in the narthex, which was actually built by Kaloyan. There are scenes from the life of St. Nicholas at the west end of the narthex, which has two floors. The lower is a small, dark chamber, which communicates with the church to the east by a narrow door; paintings in the upper one, if they exist, await cleaning. The inscriptions are all in Slav, but the iconography is completely Byzantine and the paintings are essentially Byzantine works. They show the progress of "Revival" ideas to a very marked degree. First, as in Yugoslavia, the donor portraits have an important part to play, and were obviously done from the life. Second, the figures of the Bible scenes are unusually expressive and "humanist". Third, the work is of very high quality. Outstanding among the figures are those of our Lord in practically every scene where He is present. The conception of Him as a youth in the scene where He disputes with the doctors in the Temple is unusual, and what strikes most, perhaps, is the sheer beauty of His face (*Byzantine Art*, pl. 21). But the doctors themselves are also all particularly expressive and life-like, and each one is an individual.[1] The conception of Christ at a more mature age, as in the Pantocrator in the dome or where He is shown enthroned, blessing, is no less expressive and alive, but at the same time more profound (Pl. 44, *a*). Relationship with the work in Sancta Sophia at Ochrid nearly two centuries earlier is apparent, especially in the blessing Christ. In the Bible scenes, eastern elements are present in the iconography and in the

---

[1] The coloured plates in G. Stoikov, *Boyana Church, Studies in Bulgaria's Architectural Heritage*, Sofia, 1954, serve to give a good idea of the quality of this work.

style; thus our Lord's body in the Crucifixion is severely dis-
torted, and there is a marked lack of suavity in such scenes as
the Transfiguration, which at times is almost "expressionist".

Wherever the influences come from, however, new ideas are
present, and it is perhaps best to regard Boiana as representing
a reaction of the Slav spirit and of the new ideas which were
general in the later twelfth and thirteenth centuries upon the
monastic style as we see it, for example, in such a monument as
Hosios Lukas in Greece, rather than upon the refined style of
Constantinople that we see in the mosaics of Sancta Sophia or
in the scenes at Daphni. The white high-lights and subtle
colour reflexes that characterise the Constantinopolitan school,
as for example in the portrait of Alexios Comnenos in Sancta
Sophia, are absent; instead the modelling is achieved by carefully graded tones of a rather sombre colour. Where gold or
yellow are used to accentuate the high-lights, the colours take
the form of a central splodge from which lines radiate like rays
of glory; they do not form a subtle rhythmic basis to the
modelling as in Greek work. Each scene is conceived as an
entity, elaborately composed, with full landscape or architectural backgrounds. The costumes are often richly bejewelled.
The faces are rounded, the eyes large and the intention to
express emotion is quite obvious. In the portrait of the donor,
the Sevastocrator Kaloyan, in the narthex, the intention to
produce a living and effective portrait is equally clear. The face
is subtly modelled and the drawing sure. It is a work of real
quality.

The same approach is to be found in a Bulgarian Gospel in
the British Museum, known as the Curzon manuscript; it shows
us that Bulgarian art on a small scale was just as distinct from
the Constantinopolitan as that on a large. It was perhaps done
in the region of Sofia, for the work that survives in other
places is of a different type. Thus some twelfth century paintings
at Bačkovo show a very conservative manner; they would seem
to be modelled on the mosaic of Ezechiel's vision in the
Panaghia tou Latomou (Hosios David) at Salonica (p. 95).[1]
Thirteenth century work at Tirnovo is again quite distinct.

Tirnovo was one of the most flourishing towns in the country
at this time, but little survives there owing to the violent
destructions resulting from the Turkish conquest. The earliest

[1] P. Schweinfurth, *Die Byzantinische Form*, Berlin, 1943, p. 92.

work, in the church of the Forty Martyrs, is to be assigned to the later thirteenth century. It shows a marked feeling for plasticity, and the colours were put on with a large brush in thick splodges. In the fourteenth century paintings, notably those in the church of Sts. Peter and Paul, the work is more stylised, and many of the faces are mere repetitions of others; there are few hints here of the individual portrait-like faces so characteristic of Boiana. Indeed, it is the rather formal compositions that constitute the most effective aspect of these wall paintings; they are impressive as rhythmical compositions rather than because of the sympathy or humanism of the figures or the beauty of the colouring.

Not dissimilar from, but from the artistic point of view a good deal finer than, the Tirnovo paintings are some, of the fourteenth century, in the church of St. George at Sofia. Links with Constantinople are obvious here. The work is polished and refined and shows great feeling for sweeping rhythmical composition. The colouring too has something of the brilliance and delicacy of the mosaics at Kahrieh Cami. Unfortunately only a small portion of this fine decoration survives.

Some paintings at Zemen, done about 1350, and others at Ljutibrod, done at much the same date, are of a far more eastern type, both as regards style and iconography; the tradition here would seem to stem quite definitely from Anatolia; it shows little hint of the subtler manner of the Byzantine "Revival". It would seem indeed that the old monastic tradition was very powerful in Bulgaria, and that it exercised a greater influence on work of a more advanced type than was the case in Serbia or Greece. The eastern elements in the work at Tirnovo and Sofia, to which we have already alluded, were probably introduced thanks to the presence on Bulgarian soil of such essentially eastern works as Zemen. And it is also possible that decorations of the monastic school in Serbia, like those at Marko and Lesnovo, also owe something to the influence of the Bulgarian paintings. The eastern features at Zemen are to be seen in iconography, colouring and composition alike; the approach is realist, though the painter was not always able to achieve the effects he sought; he was an able copyist rather than a master of original distinction. His work may be contrasted with that at Vodoća, of the later thirteenth century, where the scene of the Forty Martyrs is rendered with profound feeling and emotion.[1] The agony of each of the martyrs is here expressed in a truly personal way, and the whole picture is profoundly moving. A Byzantine model, perhaps an ivory, must have been followed closely, but a new personality and expression has entered in, compatible with the outlook of the Byzantine "Revival". Some fourteenth century painting at Berende must also be noted. It is decorative rather than profound, but some of the compositions are of quality. The work must have been inspired from Serbia and was perhaps even done by a Serbian painter.

Before leaving the Balkans, a word should be said about Roumania. The first influences came from Bulgaria, for Roumania took over the Bulgar church language in the eleventh century, and ties between the two countries remained important. There were schools for the Bulgarian version of the Slav language in the Roumanian monasteries until the sixteenth century, and Slav was the cultured as well as the religious language under the Turkish domination. So far as art was concerned, the Bulgarian influence was counteracted to some extent by the development of an active local school in Wallacia, Moldavia and the Bucovinà, and by direct contacts with Constantinople, exemplified in the presence of Byzantine painters, who used Greek for their inscriptions, and Byzantine ecclesiastics; a bishop was thus nominated to Wallacia from Constantinople in 1359.

On these foundations a number of flourishing local schools were built up, and some very extensive decorations, on the outsides as well as the insides of churches, remain. There is, however, little in the country that is to be dated before the fifteenth century, except for some fourteenth century work in the church of St. Nicholas at Curtea Arges. The inscriptions are in Greek and the paintings were probably done by a master from Constantinople; the iconography is close to that of the Kahrieh mosaics.[2] Some of the individual figures are particularly fine. Of the fifteenth century paintings the most important are those at Popauti (1496), Bistrita (1498), St. Nicholas of Dorohoi, Voronets and Redauti, all done towards the end of the century. Many of these paintings, especially those on the outsides of the

[1] K. Miatev, "Les 40 Martyrs: fragment de fresque à Vodoća". *L'Art byzantin chez les Slaves*, I, p. 102.

[2] O. Tafrali, *Monuments Piot*, XXIII, 1918-19.

churches, have been much restored, for Roumania enjoyed a greater degree of independence and prosperity under Turkish rule than did the other Balkan countries or Greece, and in the sixteenth century painters from other areas seem to have sought work and refuge there. There must have been quite an influx of painters from Serbia at this time. Though it is well preserved and extensive, most of this Roumanian work has the character of "folk" rather than "fine" art, and it must take a secondary place in a survey which is concerned in the main with work of high artistic quality.

BOOKS

G. Millet and D. Talbot Rice, *Byzantine Painting at Trebizond*, London, 1936.

S. Radojćić and D. Talbot Rice, *Yugoslavia—Mediaeval Frescoes*, Unesco World Art Series, 1955.

A. Grabar, *La Peinture religieuse en Bulgarie*, Paris, 1928.

N

CHAPTER XV

LATER BYZANTINE PAINTING IN GREECE

ONLY one major monument of Byzantine art of the early fourteenth century survives at Constantinople, namely the mosaic decoration of a small church on the confines of the city, usually known by its Turkish name of Kahrieh Cami. Here, in the inner and outer narthices, is preserved a rich series of mosaics, which were set up soon after 1310, thanks to the generosity of a local noble, Theodore Metochites by name. These mosaics certainly constitute one of the most glorious productions of a very productive century, but like so many of the finest examples of Byzantine art they can be fully enjoyed only by those who are lucky enough to see them on the spot, since their brilliant scintillating colours are one of their greatest glories. But, nevertheless, something of the delicacy of line of the drawing, the subtlety of expression of the figures, the vividness of the scenes and the great beauty of the compositions as a whole can be gauged from a monochrome reproduction. The mosaics of the two narthices are devoted to the lives of Christ and the Virgin, which are told in a full cycle of scenes. Typical is a fullness of detail and a severity of composition, which at first seems to give an effect of formalism. Yet the humanistic touch of the Revival style is to be seen clearly in the character of the faces and in the attitudes of the figures; this is especially clear in small scenes such as the detail of the washing of the Child in the Nativity or in the seated figure of Joseph, who waits with pensive expectancy for news of the birth of the Infant (Pl. 45). Typical of the period to which the mosaics belong is the extensive use of light-coloured high-lights; they are especially prominent in the costumes of the angels. But it is not only in the brilliance of their colouring and the delightful quality of the detail that the Kahrieh mosaics stand out; they also show tender humanism, combined with a grandeur which was at one time held to be typical only of work done before the Latin conquest. This is especially marked with regard to a great panel showing the Virgin interceding with our Lord. It was once thought to be of the twelfth century, but recent cleaning has disclosed two further figures of donors and an inscription which establishes a date around 1310 beyond dispute.[1]

Not all the panels have quite this dignity and majesty, but in their place is to be found a new interest in vivid detail, and if grandeur is sometimes absent, there are fresh qualities of liveliness, delicacy and exquisite beauty to compensate for it. Nowhere is this more apparent than in the details of the scene of the Dormition of the Virgin, which stands in the main body of the church immediately above the western door. The cubes of the mosaic are small, and are set with great care and skill. The colours are astonishingly lovely, and the modelling subtle and effective. The way in which it is achieved by the use of high-lights is particularly striking. To appreciate the richness and excellence of the art to the full, it is necessary to study the technique in detail. The faces of the Apostles who stand behind the Virgin's bier are perhaps the most striking individual works in the church.

No less important than the mosaics of Kahrieh is the painted decoration of a side aisle, which is now in the process of being cleaned by the Byzantine Institute of America. In the apse is a great Anastasis—the scene where Christ descends to hell and raises up Adam from the grave, which was in the Byzantine world always used to depict the Resurrection. In the dome is a bust of the Virgin supported by angels, and on the walls and the rest of the roof are scenes from the Old Testament. These paintings are of the very highest quality; indeed they are fully worthy to be compared with the almost exactly contemporary work of Giotto in the Arena chapel at Padua. The massiveness and monumentality of Giotto's work is absent, and the paintings are two- rather than three-dimensional. But the Kahrieh work is nevertheless more profoundly spiritual as well as perhaps more exquisite in quality.

Many such monuments, in paint if not in mosaic, must once have graced the churches of Constantinople, but now vestiges survive in only two churches, where there are fragments of the mosaic decorations; they are the Pammakaristos, usually known

---

[1] P. A. Underwood, "The Deesis mosaics in the Kahrieh Cami at Istanbul", in *Late Classical and Mediaeval Studies in Honor of A. M. Friend*, Ed. K. Weitzmann Princeton, 1955.

by its Turkish name of Fetiyeh Cami, and St. Teodore Tyro, better known as Kilisse Cami. The mosaics in the former are close in style to those of Kahrieh, though the work is a good deal less distinguished; the latter are coarser in technique, though not ineffective. Other decorations perhaps lie hidden below replasterings in other churches which have been converted into mosques.

Outside Constantinople there are a few paintings which serve to give an idea of the quality of the best fourteenth century work, in spite of the poor condition into which the churches that contain them have usually fallen. Most important is a series of mosaics only recently discovered in the dome and on the vaults of the church of the Holy Apostles at Salonica, dated to about 1312. Technically they are of much the same quality as the work at Kahrieh, but the colouring is paler in tone and the style completely distinct, for whereas Kahrieh is idealistic, delicate and static, the work at Salonica is realistic, vivid and more dynamic. The figures of the shepherds in the Nativity are typical; they seem to be portraits from the life; the startled attitudes of the two men have been rendered by the artist in a most expressive manner, and the whole scene is full of a detail more lively but less decorative than at Kahrieh.

Xyngopoulos regards these mosaics as typifying a distinct school, allied to, but different from, that of Constantinople.[1] It is to be equated with the school distinguished by Millet as the Macedonian, which probably had its main centre at Salonica, though apart from the mosaics in the church of the Holy Apostles, some wall paintings in the same building and others in the chapel of St. Euthemios in the church of St. Demetrius, little survives there. But there are a number of monuments elsewhere, some in Greece and some in what is to-day Yugoslavia, to which attention has already been called (see p. 185). They were probably all done by Greek painters, two of whom, Michael and Eutychios, we know by name. There are paintings of the same style at Kastoria and Verria, and in a number of the monastery churches on Mount Athos. The most outstanding of them is the decoration in the church of the Protaton at Karyes on Mount Athos. It was done for Andronicos II, and must date from around 1300. A few fragments remain in their original condition, but the main area of

---

[1] *Thessalonique et la peinture macédonienne*, Athens, 1955.

Constantinople. Kahrieh Camì Mosaic: the Nativity. c. 1310. (*Photo Powel.*)

PLATE 45

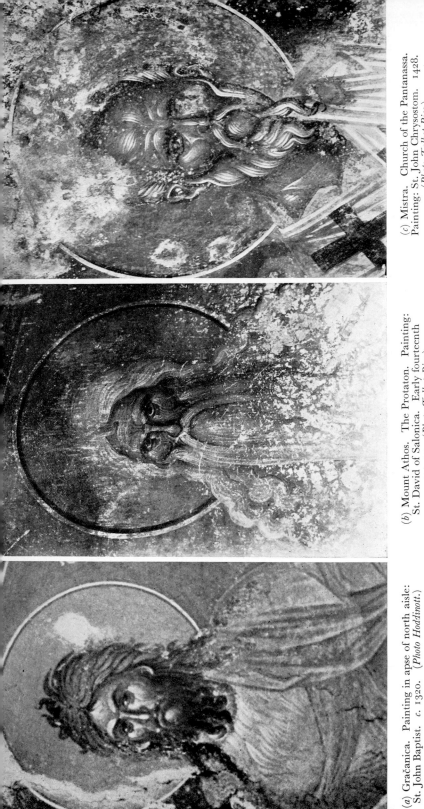

(a) Gračanica. Painting in apse of north aisle: St. John Baptist. c. 1320. (Photo Hoddinott.)

(b) Mount Athos. The Protaton. Painting: St. David of Salonica. Early fourteenth century. (Photo Talbot Rice.)

(c) Mistra. Church of the Pantanassa. Painting: St. John Chrysostom. 1428. (Photo Talbot Rice.)

PLATE 46

the decoration was retouched in the sixteenth century. Happily this did not affect the design or colouring very seriously, so that the whole decoration may virtually be assigned to that date. Quite recently additional work has been discovered which was obscured by an eighteenth century roof. All is very close indeed to the style of the paintings in the chapel of St. Euthemios in the church of St. Demetrius at Salonica which are dated 1303.

The Protaton paintings have long been associated with the name of a painter especially renowned in Greek tradition, namely Panselinos. There has been a great deal of argument regarding the date at which this man worked, and he has normally been regarded as a sixteenth century painter. Xyngopoulos has shown, however, that there seems good reason to follow an old legend associating him with the Protaton paintings. Their similarity to the work of 1303 at Salonica proves their early date, and, if he is correct, Panselinos can thus be accepted as the principal master of the early Macedonian school. His name has survived, though he does not seem to have signed his work. But other painters did so, and by soon after 1300 the habit of signing had become quite usual all over the Byzantine world. It is just another indication of the change of outlook, which is also exemplified in the greater realism and humanism of the paintings themselves.

Of the Protaton paintings, the New Testament cycle is very complete and is typical of the style of the master. It is personal and distinctive. The figures are massive and well modelled, the expressions are profound, the colouring rather sombre and heavy, with deep greys, mauves and greens predominating. The figure of St. David of Salonica may serve as an example (Pl. 46, *b*). The architectural backgrounds which were so popular in much of the work of the fourteenth century are present when conservatism or convention demand, but there is less profusion of detail of this sort than, for instance, at Kahrieh, and in many cases the architecture is omitted altogether, so that the figures are shown virtually in silhouette. Realism is the hall-mark of the style, and if it is less decorative and in many ways less attractive than the Cretan manner which followed it, it is also more profound.

In addition to his work in the Protaton at Karyes, Panselinos also painted a church in the monastery of Russikon, but it

was pulled down in the nineteenth century to make room for a
larger and more ambitious building. Exactly where else he
worked is uncertain, but some of the paintings at Vatopedi are
in a style very closely similar to those of the Protaton, and they
are certainly to be assigned to his school if not to the master
himself. The figure of Christ in the scene of the Washing of the
Apostles' Feet may be compared with the Christ in the
Protaton. But the work at Vatopedi is much later, for it is to
be dated around 1550, and if Panselinos was really a fourteenth
century master, the similarity is perhaps to be attributed to the
effects of restoration in the Protaton. This sixteenth century
work represents the last great accomplishment of a very old
tradition. But if the work on Athos was still distinguished in the
sixteenth century, elsewhere decadence had set in, and on the
whole Byzantine wall painting of this age was not of very high
quality.

A second extremely important series of paintings, which were
also regarded as examples of the Macedonian school by Millet,
exists at Mistra in the Peloponnese. It is to be questioned, however, whether any of the work there was really Macedonian;
it seems to be allied more closely to Constantinople than to
Salonica, and this holds for the more advanced as well as the
more conservative trends. The earliest of the paintings there
are some in the church of St. Demetrius, also known as the
Metropolis, which were done in 1310. But though they were
painted by a master of great ability, in practically the same
year that the mosaics of Kahrieh were executed, they are in a
more conservative style and represent the survival in the fourteenth century of the monumental manner typical of the earlier
mosaics, like those of Daphni near Athens. Much of the work
in St. Demetrius is of great dignity, notably the Virgin in the
eastern apse. It is, however, probably the colouring of the
paintings in this church that attracts the attention most, and its
effect can even be appreciated to some extent in a monochrome
reproduction, for example in the bands of varied shades used
for the rainbowlike glories in the most sacred of the scenes.
They serve to give a fine impression of celestial power and a
great feeling of space.

A second painter who worked in the same church some
twenty years later possessed a more personal, more intimate
style, closer to that of the Kahrieh mosaics; the most striking

feature of his work is the great elaboration of the architectural backgrounds, done in bright, contrasting colours. But he also used high-lights with great effect; they were put on in large splashes, above the darker tones of faces and costumes.

The same painter, or one whose style was closely similar, was responsible for some work done about 1360 in the church of the Brontocheion, also known as the Aphentico. Unfortunately this is one of the most seriously damaged churches at Mistra, but two compositions survive in comparatively good preservation, a pair of angels in an inner chamber, and a bust of the Prophet Melchizedek in what is left of the main body of the church. The Prophet is particularly noteworthy (Pl. 44, *b*). The drawing is finished and delicate, and the modelling, with the sharply defined high-lights, is forceful and imaginative, and the colouring superb; though entirely non-naturalistic—green being used for the hair, for example—nothing could be more effective or more inspiring. The naturalistic manner that we saw at Mileševa has here given place to what is really a form of symbolism, and the aesthetic approach of the Mistra painter would seem to have been close to that of the modern artist. The essential difference is that the Mistra works were at heart basically Christian, and were inspired by faith. Often indeed they seem the very embodiment of faith in visual form.

A similar style predominated in the decoration of another church at Mistra, the Pantanassa, though it was done in the next century, actually around the year 1428. Happily the church at least has a roof, and even if many of the paintings are terribly damaged, an extensive series of New Testament scenes is available for study. Several hands must have been responsible for their execution. One man, who did a medallion of the Virgin and Child in a small dome at the western end, took particular delight in formalistic pattern, and even where the rays of glory which play so important a part in these paintings were not called for, he seems to have made his compositions as formal as possible. This is clearly apparent in the modelling of the figures of the Apostles on the south wall, or in the way in which the high-lights were applied to the face of St. John Chrysostom (Pl. 46, *c*). The primary object in applying the high-lights was doubtless to build up the modelling of the face, but they seem in addition to play an even more important part as elements of the formal composition as a whole. Their role is, in fact, very similar to that of the crosses and patterns which are so important a part of the Saint's ecclesiastical vestment.

The hand of another artist in the same church is to be distinguished by the interest he took in detail, and more especially in the detail of the architectural backgrounds. This is clearly obvious in the scenes of the main New Testament cycle, like the Raising of Lazarus or the Presentation in the Temple; both scenes are enacted before backgrounds almost as elaborate as a stage set. The architectural backgrounds derive directly from the architecturescapes of Pompeian and Hellenistic art, and the painter at Mistra must have followed an old model closely, even though he elaborated on it. The apse of the temple in the Presentation scene, for instance, looks almost like one of the façades of Petra, except that it is rather more elaborate.

Yet, with all this love of formalism on the one hand and decorative detail on the other, the artists who adorned the Pantanassa never lost sight of the main object of art, and each picture remains a thing of beauty in itself, and exists as a vehicle for the interpretation of the spirit of the scene. If this picture had been a panel by Giotto, thousands of pounds would have been paid for it in an auction room. As it is a wall painting by an unknown Greek, it is allowed to perish and moulder, without any serious effort being made to preserve it. The callous neglect with which the Greeks have treated these monuments of the artistic past of their country is indeed astonishing, and is in marked contrast to the care that has been lavished on kindred monuments in Yugoslavia.

Attention has already been drawn to the interest in architectural backgrounds that characterises the work of many of the painters of the fourteenth and early fifteenth centuries, and we have noted the presence of these backgrounds at Kahrieh as well as in the Pantanassa at Mistra. Though the models from which they were taken date from early times, however, the backgrounds themselves passed out of favour in the intermediary period, and in work of the twelfth century they were as often as not absent. Thus at Nerezi in 1164 the figures were placed before backgrounds on which only the more essential features of the scenes are indicated, such as the cross in the scene of the Deposition. At Mileševa and Sopoćani a hunderd years later the backgrounds were already beginning to become crowded, though with a mass of figures rather than with architectural detail. At Kahrieh Cami, about 1310, architectural compositions, on the other hand, played an important part, while in the Pantanassa at Mistra, after the lapse of a further century, profusion of architectural detail has almost become the hallmark of the work. Indeed, these later backgrounds sometimes cease to be purely conventional and take on the character of vivid views of some contemporary town, as seen from a distance, in which the tall roofs of houses, the domes of churches, and the towers of castles can be distinguished.

With this change in the character and composition of the backgrounds there went a similar change of outlook regarding the number of subsidiary figures, the details of costumes and so on. In the Entry into Jerusalem at the Pantanassa, for example, there are trees and buildings in the foreground, and the main figures show a dynamic quality hardly ever present at an earlier date. The small boys who cast down their cloaks in our Lord's path thus have the vivid energy of street urchins; they are not simply conventional figures culled from some ancient manuscript model. The same liveliness and realism is to be observed in the scene of the Annunciation, where the Angel hovers before a background so full of detail that it is almost uneasy, while in the foreground there is a little fountain with two partridges drinking at it (Pl. 48, a). Charming though it is, this realism and love of detail tends at times to detract from the religious significance of the composition. It is this that distinguishes the provincial style from that of Constantinople.

This tendency towards the stressing of detail is to be seen to an even more marked degree in the paintings of another church at Mistra, the Peribleptos, which must be dated to between 1340 and 1360. But here, though the backgrounds are full, it is the miniature-like character of the actual technique that is most striking. The figure of St. John Chrysostom is typical (Pl. 48, b). The face is executed with the minuteness of a manuscript illumination or small panel painting, and every stitch of the embroidery on the vestments is indicated. The work still has definite majesty, but it is clear that the continuance along this road towards greater minuteness would eventually lead to decadence, for the artist would inevitably become concerned with the exactitude of detailed representation rather than with the essence of form.

The manner of the Peribleptos paintings is indeed so distinctive that Millet regarded them as the forerunners of a new school which he termed the Cretan. There are, however, but few manifestations of it in Crete itself, and what there are are all late in date, so that the name is not a very satisfactory one.[1] The style actually reached its highest development on the mainland of Greece from the fifteenth century onwards and on Mount Athos in the sixteenth century. It spread, moreover, to the Balkans, and such paintings as those at Kalenić (1405-1410), Ljubostinja (1405), Rudenića (c. 1410) and Poganovo (c. 1500) in Yugoslavia may be noted (see p. 187 f.). There are even more examples of slightly later date in Roumania, though few of them are of any great artistic significance.

The style reached its most characteristic and most important stage of development in a number of churches on Mount Athos. Most striking perhaps are the paintings in the old church at Xenophontos, executed by a painter named Anthony about 1544 (*Byzantine Art*, pl. 23). His style is characterised by the use of severely stressed high-lights, put on in broad, sweeping strokes. The scene of the Sleeping Apostles in the Garden shows this clearly. The high-lights have here become what would be called in modern parlance "symbols", and the composition of the picture has been achieved as much by their interplay as by the disposition of the actual figures. The scene is additionally interesting, in that it shows our Lord no less than three times; He goes up to the mountain to pray, He witnesses the vision from heaven, and He chides the Apostles for not keeping awake.

Another interesting example of the work of this same painter is to be seen in the Presentation in the Temple in the same church. The high-lights are here stressed less violently, and the work is consequently less individualistic; it is in fact in closer accord with the characteristic sixteenth century developments of the Cretan school which we have already traced in their early stages at Mistra. The great precision of detail, the small heads and the clear definition of the architectural backgrounds are all typical of the style and to some extent also of the age, for painting in Russia at this time tended to develop along the same lines.

[1] Earlier paintings in Crete are in the "Macedonian" style; see M. Chatzidakis, "La Peinture de la Macédoine et de la Crète", in *Proceedings of the Ninth International Congress of Byzantine Studies*, Athens, 1955.

There are rather earlier, but less individualistic, paintings in the refectory of the same monastery, done in 1512, and in the main church (1535) and the chapel of St. Nicholas at the Lavra (1560); the refectory and the main church of Dionysiou (1547), the chapel of St. George, in the monastery of St. Paul (1555), and the church (1568) and the refectory (late sixteenth century) at Docheriou also all contain more or less complete decorations of this period. Much of the work has been overpainted and restored at subsequent dates, usually with disastrous results, but even so, something of the quality of the old designs remains, so that the original appearance is indicated perhaps more clearly in a photograph, where the unpleasant colours of the restoration are not there to shock the eye. This is, for example, very much the case at Chilandari. The main church or Catholicon there was decorated in 1302, and here and there a few paintings, notably a portrait of one of the monasteries' principal benefactors, King Milutin, survive untouched. But most of the work, including the whole of the very extensive New Testament cycle, was entirely restored in 1804. The colours of this restoration are repulsive, and the texture of the paint most unpleasant, but the original iconographical scheme has been preserved almost exactly, and something of the fine, sweeping line of the original design is also present.

Apart from the effects of restorations, these paintings are also often difficult to see, and still more difficult to photograph, owing to the inaccessibility of their positions in the monastic churches, which are usually ill-lit and invariably filled up with a mass of subsidiary furnishings. It is in the smaller chapels, which are usually more sparsely furnished and where the paintings can be studied close at hand, that their qualities can be best appreciated. Most interesting of these is the small chapel dedicated to St. George, in the monastery of St. Paul, the decoration of which was done in 1555. It is a tiny building, high up on the monastery wall, but every inch of its interior is covered with paintings, which comprise portraits of saints either full length or in medallions, and a number of scenes from the New Testament. The subtlety of the best work of the early fourteenth century is, no doubt, absent, but the painter who worked in this chapel had a good sense of design, and he adapted his compositions with very great skill to the rather awkward spaces that were in many cases the only ones available. Each scene is treated as a separate picture, and is framed by a bright red border. The backgrounds are full and elaborate, yet there is great feeling for formal pattern. The colours are bright and pleasant, and high-lights are used with great effect. The scene of the Presentation of the child Virgin in the Temple is typical of the work, and shows all these features. But the most beautiful of all the scenes is probably that of the Transfiguration, where the figure of Christ is fine and expressive, and where the formal pattern of the Glory before which He stands is in itself a thing of great beauty, especially in its colour.

Another instance of good work on a small scale is to be found in a diminutive chapel at Karyes, dedicated to St. John the Baptist, or rather St. John Prodromos, the Forerunner, as he is usually known in the Orthodox world. The symbol of the Holy Spirit, in the form of a dove with spread wings, is shown in a medallion adjacent to an impressive figure of God the Father (Fig. 21). The date of these paintings has been disputed. Robert Byron, convinced by the excellence of the design and the expressive power of some of the figures, thought that the work must date from the fourteenth century, even if it had been considerably overpainted at a later time. Millet, following an inscription, dated the paintings to 1701.[1]

The figures are majestic, and the way in which the costumes of some of them, notably the Prophet Noah, are done certainly suggests an early date. But these figures are, as far as technique is concerned, in the same paint and the same manner as the rest of the work, and it seems hardly possible to assign the more conservative portions of the painting to one age and the details, like the sprigs that decorate God the Father's costume, to another. In fact, we would seem to be in the presence of a very unusual decoration, but of one which is uniform. The form of the letters in which the titles of the scenes and the names of the figures are written, the character of the costumes and the decorative details all savour of the late seventeenth or the early eighteenth century, and there can hardly be any doubt but that the inscription gives the correct date. The paintings serve to show that the old tradition had not entirely died out even by the eighteenth century, and though most of the wall paintings of this later age were either some-

---

[1] *The Birth of Western Painting*, 1930, p. 119. Paintings in the chapel of the Prodromos are illustrated on pls. 8, 10, 11, 28, 29 and 30.

Panel: the Virgin and Child, saints and scenes from the New Testament.
Benaki Museum, Athens.   Fifteenth century.   (*Photo Museum.*)

PLATE 47

(b) Mistra. The Peribleptos. Painting: St. John Chrysostom. 1340-1360. (*Photo Talbot Rice.*)

(a) Mistra. The Pantanassa. Painting: Angel of the Annunciation. 1428. (*Photo Talbot Rice.*)

PLATE 48

FIG. 21. Chapel of the Prodromos, Karyes, Mount Athos.
Detail of wall painting. Probably 1701.

what monotonously illustrative, like those of the monasteries of the Meteora, or banal and crude, like many in the smaller churches of Greece, there were nevertheless occasional flashes of real quality. A close parallel to the wall paintings in the chapel of the Prodromos is afforded by an icon in the writer's possession bearing St. John the Baptist and St. Marina. It has been shown in several exhibitions and would have passed in any of them as a fifteenth century panel had it not borne the date 1741.

BOOKS

G. MILLET, *Monuments byzantins de Mistra*, Paris, 1910.

G. MILLET, *Monuments de l'Athos*, Paris, 1927.

R. BYRON and D. TALBOT RICE, *The Birth of Western Painting*, London, 1930.

CHAPTER XVI

PANEL PAINTING IN THE BYZANTINE WORLD

ANY book dealing with Christian art in the West would inevitably have been concerned to a considerable extent with paintings on a small scale, on panel or on canvas. Here, however, with two or three outstanding exceptions, like the Madonna in Sta Maria Novella at Rome or Our Lady of Vladimir, what are usually termed "easel pictures" have hardly been mentioned. They were nevertheless important—more important, probably, than the few examples that survive would suggest, and a short final chapter has therefore been added to deal with the panels, or "icons" as they are usually called, even though the book is otherwise arranged according to a chronological rather than a technological system. The iconography of the scenes and figures shown on the icons is identical with that of the wall paintings; the actual style and of course the technique were distinct. Technique showed but little variation throughout the centuries, and with the exception of a few early works done in the encaustic method—that is, by the manipulation of coloured waxes with a hot wire or iron—the manner of painting upon panel remained remarkably constant in the East Christian area from the seventh century till the seventeenth. The panel was coated with fine gesso; almost invariably canvas was laid over this, and worked firmly down into the gesso; a second coat of gesso was then laid above the canvas. This was polished, and the paint was then laid directly upon it. In the best work the backgrounds were overlaid with gold leaf. Indeed, occasionally the whole panel was covered in this way and the painting was done on top of the gold, but this was not usual. Nor were the gold backgrounds by any means universal, and in later times they were quite frequently done in paint only, first in yellow to imitate gold, and then in other colours, notably blue, brown or green; sometimes, especially in Russia in the fifteenth century, they were left plain, the polished gesso by itself producing a very effective background.

The very earliest panels that survive are mostly in the encaustic technique; the most outstanding examples came from the monastery on Mount Sinai and are now in the Theological Academy at Kiev; a few of them are probably to be assigned to the sixth or even to the fifth century. The style is "expressionist" and savours of the East; it is closely akin to that of the mummy portraits of Ptolemaic Egypt, and these no doubt exercised a strong influence on the earliest panels. Sinai itself was not far removed from Egypt, and as we have already noted, there were close contacts between Syria and Palestine on the one hand and Egypt on the other. The work may have actually been done at the Sinai monastery, which seems to have been an important centre of art in early times. There are some other encaustic panels still in the monastery itself which are probably to be dated to the seventh century.

Of works in actual paint the earliest is the lid of a reliquary from the Sancta Sanctorum in the Lateran, which has already been noted (Pl. 11—see p. 35). The work is primitive, not dissimilar from that of some of the Catacomb paintings, though the figures are more squat, and the eyes done in the forceful, deeply set fashion characteristic of the East. Some panels in the Sinai monastery are not dissimilar, though they are probably rather later in date.[1]

More spectacular than this tiny panel is the lovely Madonna now in the church of Sta Maria Novella at Rome (Pl. C). The face is subtly modelled, and the tones merge gently one into another, in the same way that they do in the lovely wall painting of the angel in Sta Maria Antiqua (Pl. 40, a). Especially noteworthy are the delicate pink flesh tones over a green undercoat. Green undercoats of the type that we first see here were to continue in use till very late times in art of the "transcendental" style. They were thus used by miniature and panel painters in the Byzantine world, in wall paintings in the Balkans, and by Cimabue and Duccio in Italy, not to mention their occurrence in Ottonian miniatures and Romanesque wall paintings. Their employment is recommended both in the Byzantine "Painters' Guide" and in the *Diversarium Artium*

---

[1] For reproduction of the very extensive collection of icons still in the Sinai monastery see G. Sotiriou, *Les Icones de Sinai*, Athens, 1956.

Schedula of Theophilus. It has been suggested that the colour
was first favoured because of a symbolic significance deriving
from Egypt, where green was the colour of the other world and
was associated with Osiris.[1] But by the time we see it in these
panels such symbolical ideas, if they ever existed, had probably
been forgotten, and the popularity of the method was due
primarily to technical reasons.

The position that the Virgin assumes on the Sta Maria
Novella panel is also one that was to have a very long history.
It is that which was later to become familiar as the Hodegitria,
or "Indicator of the Way". The Virgin supports the Child on
one arm and points to Him with the other across her breast.
It is likely that in this respect restorations followed the original
painting exactly, though it is only in the face of the Madonna
that the original work actually survives in an untouched state.

A panel in the Louvre, depicting Christ and a saint, and
another in the Kaiser Friedrich Museum at Berlin, showing a
sainted bishop, are perhaps a little earlier in date—they arc
usually assigned to the sixth century.[2] They are, also, far
more primitive, and belong to the same eastern school as the
encaustic panels from Sinai. Both the panels came from Egypt,
and they may best be compared with the wall paintings at
Saqqara and Baouit (see p. 43). They are indeed the forerunners of the comparatively numerous paintings in that more
primitive style that we know as Coptic.[3]

Apart from a few more examples akin to these Egyptian
works, there is little that survives from before the days of
Iconoclasm, and there are still but few paintings that can be
attributed to the ninth, tenth or eleventh centuries. A second
reliquary in the Vatican, bearing an incised cross with double
traverse and figures of Sts. Peter and Paul below, Christ and
the Virgin at the top, and archangels on either side in the
middle, is probably to be assigned to the eleventh century. It
shows work of a very distinguished character, and would seem
to have been done in the Byzantine world, perhaps at Constantinople itself. Some panels at Rome, Carpagnano and Tivoli,
published by Wilpert,[4] are on the other hand mostly to be

[1] See W. de Gruneisen, *Sta Maria Antiqua*, Rome, 1911, p. 29.
[2] Peirce and Tyler, II, pl. 166.
[3] See for example M. T. Langdon, *The Icons of Yuhanna and Ibrahim the Scribe*,
London, 1946.
[4] *Die Romischen Mosaiken und Malereien*, pls. 226, 244, 260, 263 and 271-4.

O

assigned to Italian painters, though in most cases Byzantine influence was marked and in a few the paintings may even have been done by Greeks working on Italian soil. Similarly a fine painting on silk in the church of St. Just at Trieste is Byzantine in style, though the inscription that accompanies it is in Latin (Pl. 30, *b*). The work was probably done in Italy in the eleventh century. But there is little else from the great middle period of Byzantine art; still less is there anything that can be assigned indisputably to Constantinople.

With the twelfth century, however, the picture changes, and this in more respects than one, for in the first place there are more examples, and in the second the new, more humanist style which was noted in the sphere of wall paintings also began to affect panels. As in the case with wall painting, however, the new manner only developed slowly, and alongside panels of the very greatest tenderness and humanism others were painted which were severe, formal and rigid. An icon of the Virgin in the Orans position in the Tretiakov Gallery at Moscow is thus monumental in character and symbolical as regards its iconography, and contrasts strongly with the tender, personal touch which characterises Our Lady of Vladimir. Yet there is every reason to assign the latter to the twelfth century, while the former is usually attributed to the thirteenth.[1]

The Virgin of Vladimir is an icon of really outstanding importance. In the first place, it is extremely beautiful, and on those grounds alone would take a very prominent place among the world's greatest works of art. And in the second place it was probably the first work to herald completely the taste and outlook of a new age, both in the subtlety of the painting and in the iconographical conception, for the type has changed from that of the monumental Hodegitria to the more personal, human and intimate pose known as the Eleousa or Virgin of Tenderness, where the Child's face is pressed against that of His Mother in an attitude of affection.

The change towards humanism is not absolutely complete, for the Virgin's left hand still indicates the Child with a gesture

---

[1] For the Orans icon see Weidlé, *Le Icone Bizantine e Russe*, Florence, 1950, pl. xix. The Virgin of Vladimir was at one time often regarded as of the eleventh century—see M. Alpatov and V. Lazarev, "Ein Byzantinisches Tafelwerk aus der Komnenenepoche", *Jahrbuch der Preuszischen Kunstsammlungen*, XLVI, 1925, p. 140. More recently a suggestion has been put forward that it is a thirteenth century copy of a twelfth century original; see p. 162.

of respect and reverence, thus showing that it is not simply a picture of a mother and child but one representing the Divine Child in human form and that the Mother is aware of His nature. In fact, an ideal compromise between the beauty of human affection and the transcendental religious approach seems to have been achieved here. It was not until much later that a conception of the Virgin as mother above all else came into art, where the gesture of reverence was abandoned. The earliest example of this type that has so far been recorded in the Byzantine world is an icon dated to 1350 at Dečani in Yugo-slavia.[1] By soon after that date the change had been achieved in Russia on a fairly extensive scale; an icon in the Tretiakov Gallery at Moscow, of the late fourteenth century, may be cited.[2] In the West the conception had altered much earlier, and we see the Virgin as a youthful and totally unspiritual figure in Gothic sculpture even in the thirteenth century; one of the most striking examples is that of the south porch at Amiens of 1288.

A few other icons survive which were probably painted in Constantinople during the twelfth century; one of St. John the Evangelist in the Loverdos collection at Athens has recently been published by Xyngopoulos[3]; it is fairly close in style to the wall paintings of St. Demetrius at Vladimir, which are dated 1195.

But it is really not until we get to the later thirteenth century that surviving icons become at all common. From that time on-wards there is an increasing wealth of material and the distinc-tion of schools becomes feasible. As yet, however, it is only with regard to panel paintings in Russia that enough work has been done to make it possible to assign works to localities beyond little question of doubt. There, in addition to icons which were imported from Constantinople or which were done by immi-grant Greeks who had retained their native style, the schools of Kiev, Novgorod and Vladimir can be distinguished at an early date, while later those of Pskov, Suzdal, Yaroslave and Moscow also developed. In Greece and the Balkans distinctions are less definite, and at the moment only a fairly broad classification

---

[1] M. Ćorović-Ljubinković, "Deux Icones de la Vierge du Monastère de Dečani", *Starinar*, III-IV, Beograd, 1952-53, p. 91.
[2] Weidlé, *loc. cit.*, pl. xxxviii.
[3] "Une Icone du temps des Comnènes", *Mélanges Henri Grégoire* (Annuaire de l'Institut de Philologie et d'Histoire, tome X), Bruxelles, 1950, II, p. 659.

is possible, similar to that used in connection with the wall paintings. Work which was done by Slavs can thus be distinguished from that done by Greeks, if only on the basis of epigraphy, and the finished, polished manner of the capital is quite distinct from the less sophisticated style of the provinces or the more primitive manner of the monasteries. And further, the vivid liveliness of the Macedonian school is distinct from the more refined style of Constantinople, which led on to the detailed, highly finished work of the Cretan school. But farther than that it is still impossible to go, and one cannot as yet associate schools with any degree of certainty with such places as Salonica or Ochrid, Mount Athos or the Greek Islands, in any case until well on into the fifteenth century.

When study of late Byzantine panel painting has progressed farther, a far more exact classification should certainly become possible; for the moment it must suffice to note two broad lines of development. The one is that associated with the Macedonian school in wall painting, where liveliness, expression and vigour are to the fore; an icon bearing the Transfiguration in the Benaki Museum at Athens may serve as an example (*Byzantine Art*, pl. 35). The other is the more refined style of the Cretan school. The icon of the Transfiguration is probably to be dated to the fifteenth century, and was perhaps painted in Salonica. It is large in scale, and expressive in character. More refined, and closer in style to what was typical of Constantinople, is an icon depicting the Crucifixion, now in the Byzantine Museum at Athens.[1] The faces have been severely damaged by scratching, but in spite of this it is possible to appreciate the quality of the work. St. John's grief is poignantly and openly expressed; our Lord's body is bent in a way that accentuates tremendously the pathetic aspect of the scene; the tall, thin figure of the Virgin, with head muffled in her cloak, is wonderfully expressive of a profound sadness which is more than personal. In other panels of quality of this school the same power of expression is there, though it is not of course always so profound an emotion that is sought but often the vivid joyousness of life, as for instance in such a scene as our Lord's Entry into Jerusalem.

The painters of the Cretan school were on the whole much

---

[1] See the catalogues of the respective museums for reproductions of these and other icons, and also the author's *Byzantine Art*, Pelican Books, 1954, pl. 35.

less interested in such emotions. Their art was more decorative, and it was in the work of this school that the distinctively Byzantine method of using light-coloured high-lights on faces and on costumes was most fully developed. These began to be used in very early times; attention has already been called to them as denoting Byzantine workmanship in the case of some of the wall paintings in Sta Maria Antiqua. But it was not until the twelfth century that this high-lighting came to be developed as a completely distinctive system. At first these high-lights take the form of thin parallel white lines, used on costumes, hair and faces alike. Then, in the thirteenth century, the lines were broken up and the lights were put on more in masses than in lines, and were used with greater discrimination on the lighted portions of face and figure only; such a usage is to be seen on the famous panels of late thirteenth or early fourteenth century date from St. Clement at Ochrid or that showing the enthroned Virgin between angels in the Accademia at Florence,[1] or one of the Virgin and Child, with scenes from the New Testament above and saints at the sides and below, in the Benaki Museum at Athens (Pl. 47). There are numerous icons in the same manner in the collections of Greece and Yugoslavia, and it should prove possible to distinguish a whole series of local groups within these major schools when study has progressed farther. And, from the fifteenth century onwards, if not before, it becomes possible to distinguish the work of individual painters also.

In Byzantine art of the great periods the individuality of the artist was invariably suppressed, for works were done under the patronage of the Emperor or the Church, to the greater glory of God, and the artist did not sign them, even if his name was known to his own age. But with the thirteenth century, as we have seen, the habit of signing paintings came in, and it gradually grew in popularity, especially in Macedonia, Serbia and Greece.

The names of certain men working on wall paintings in Macedonia have already been noted, and those of quite a number of other painters could be added to the list. It is not, however, till the fifteenth century that the names of icon painters begin to be known in any number, and not till the sixteenth that it becomes possible to put together anything like

---

[1] Weidlé, *op. cit.*, pl. XXII.

a corpus of these names.[1] The best known of these men worked in the western islands of Greece or in Venice, where there was a large Greek colony. A representative collection of their icons is preserved in the church of San Giorgio dei Greci at Venice. They are often works of great charm—but they are hardly to be termed great art, like the sculptures, wall paintings or mosaics of earlier times, or like the paintings of one such man who was born in Crete and who, like many of the others, moved to Venice. Unlike the rest, he adopted a Western style; unlike the rest, he was a man of really outstanding genius. His name was Domenicos Theotocopoulos, but we know him better by his Spanish nickname, el Greco.

BOOKS

O. WULFF and M. ALPATOV, *Denkmäler der Ikonenmalerei*, Leipzig, 1925.

W. FELICETTI-LIEBENFELS, *Geschichte der Byzantinischen Ikonenmalerei*, Lausanne, 1956.

D. TALBOT RICE, *The Icons of Cyprus*, London, 1937.

W. WEIDLÉ, *Le Icone Bizantine e Russe*, Florence, 1950.

[1] Demetrios Sisilianos, *Greek Icon-painters*, Athens, 1935 (in Greek).

ENVOI

IN some ways it seems inappropriate to end the story of early Christian art with the mention of these late icons in Venice. When dealing with the West the story was broken off at around the year 1100, when the old art was at its height and was giving way to a new one, derived to some extent from it, but which was to see more than one age of great glory in the years that were to follow. In the East we have continued the tale past the twelfth century "Revival", through the last age of glory in the early fourteenth century, down to the final periods of undoubted decadence. It may be that we should have ended it with the mosaics of Kahrieh Cami. But what followed was an intrinsic part of what went before. Late Byzantine art was not a new art, like Gothic. The old forms were to be repeated, the old ideas re-enacted for several centuries to come, and if at times the repetitions were arid, the enactments banal, they were all done not only in good faith but also in the light of old ideas. In fact, though some of the last icons of quality were painted in the seventeenth or even the eighteenth century, they were still early Christian in spirit and character. Thus with them the story reaches its legitimate close, not at an apex, as in Britain, France or Germany about 1100, but at its end. In the West in the last thirty years we have been watching the change from an old to a new idiom in art, and however much we may be amazed by some of the most recent manifestations, we feel sure that in the end something of quality will emerge. Whatever form the new art may take, whether it be representational or abstract, naturalistic or formal, there will be something there to bind the new art to the old, just as the work of Gauguin and Van Gogh is bound to that of the Impressionists, that of the Impressionists to Constable, that of Constable to Rubens. In the East Christian world, on the other hand, the story has ended; the old art is dead and can never with honesty be revived. The next phase will come by revolution, not by evolution. What form it will take we cannot say. Enough, for us, that the old art was great and that it constituted for many hundreds of years the supreme expression of faith in a large section of the civilised world.

INDEX

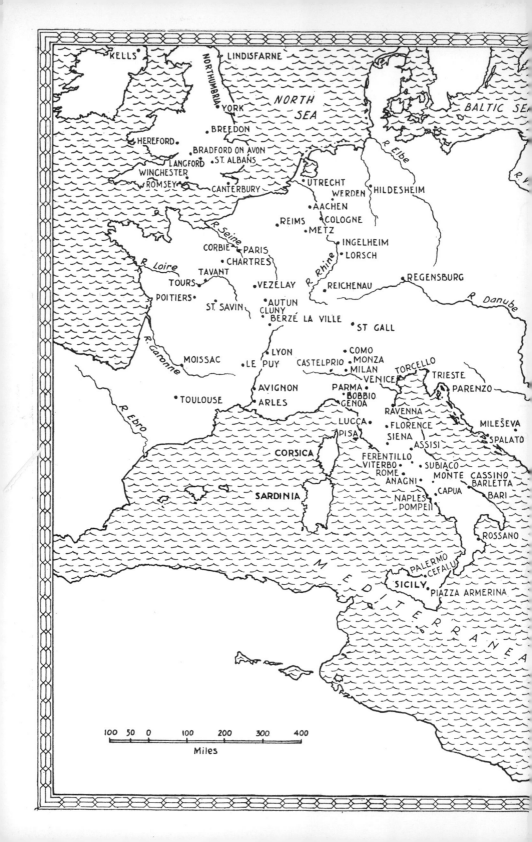